THE
LOG
HOME
PLAN
BOOK

CINDY THIEDE

WITH HEATHER MEHRA-PEDERSEN

FLOOR PLANS REDRAWN AND ILLUSTRATED BY LOG RHYTHMS AND WRIGHT DESIGN

GIBBS·SMITH
P
PUBLISHER

SALT LAKE CITY

04 03 02 01   9 8 7 6 5

Published by
Gibbs Smith, Publisher
P.O. Box 667
Layton, Utah 84041
Orders: (1-800) 748-5439
WWW.GIBBS-SMITH.COM

Design by Leesha Jones, Moon & the Stars Design
Printed and bound in Korea

LIBRARY OF CONGRESS CATALOGING-IN-PUBLICATION DATA

Thiede, Cindy Teipner, 1958-
The log home plan book / Cindy Thiede, Heather Mehra-Pedersen. —1st ed.
p.   cm.
ISBN 0-87905-922-2
1. Log cabins. I. Mehra-Pedersen, Heather. II. Title.
TH4840.T4523   1999
690'.837—dc21   99-28963
                                           CIP

CONTENTS

ACKNOWLEDGMENTS

This time, things were a little different. The idea for this fourth book on log homes took shape about the time the book was due; in other words, panic city! I missed out on the opportunity and pleasure of traveling around the country with my cameras. Instead, with a few exceptions, we drew on the talents of other photographers who I gratefully acknowledge here. Thanks to log companies everywhere who worked hand in hand with us to bring this book to print. To Lee and Greg Steckler of Log Rhythms and Rick Wright of Wright Design, thanks for coming through with quality and humor. (How 'bout it Lee, three cheers for those superwoman capes!). To my greatest supporter, Lise Mousel-Martini, who said, simply, there was time enough (and something like "go girl!")—dinner's on me. (Dear Omar, you're invited too if you promise to leave the camels at home!) Thanks to my best boys, Tyler and Jesse, and Mr. Mom (who makes that killer casserole surprise ala kitchen sink). As for my talented and very funny friend Heather, indeed, you saved the day! Thanks for venturing west when I needed you most. Ditto thanks to all those people on Heather's long list below—a support team and a little faith are everything. Special thanks to Dr. Bruce and Ron for computer support and e-mail entertainment extraordinaire :) Last, but not least: kudos to editor Madge Baird, designer Leesha Jones, and the whole crew at Gibbs Smith, Publisher—think logs!

—CINDY THIEDE

My heart of hearts goes to my ideal husband, Dr. Bruce Pedersen, who shoved me out the door to help me fulfill a dream (really, I know it was support!). Your unwavering, positive attitude and steadfast, constant belief in me instills the confidence to know "I can." Now I can say, "I did." I love and thank you so very much. (Randy and Nancy, thanks for hatching him!)

One thousand thank-yous to Helenji and Dad for your patience, tolerance, love and babysitting services while I birthed this fourth child in a quarter the term. I couldn't, and wouldn't, have possibly done it without you. Big, fat, blue hugs and kisses to Kipling, Rio and Selkirk, my three cherished piglets who generously, but reluctantly, gave me permission to spend the nights away for the cause when necessary. To my mother, Doots McGee, and closest sister, Dr. Dawn Mehra, you are the two most treasured women in my life. To Carol Seiler, friend and confidant, John Mittl, my favorite well-preserved man, and the rest of the staff at Mountain Shadow Veterinary Hospital, thank you for keeping my husband somewhat sane and the hospital monster at bay while I was temporarily indisposed. To my friends Uncle T, Ma Mish, Christa, Lisa Hos, LuAnne, Linda, Laurie, Dean the Clown, Dotes, Rusty, and Rambut, thanks for your continued support in so many different ways. Heartfelt thanks to the Byrd who kept us fed and smiling! Two kisses (with almonds) to Pat McDonald and Wendy Bullock, the FedEx team who kept our spirits high by hand delivering chocolate that absolutely, positively had to be there overnight.

And Cindy, without you, I'd have no place to put these acknowledgements! It's been an honor to work with you; you truly are a credit to your profession. Although the working quarters were tight and the hours long, we still have all of our hair, it's not gray, and your one eye doesn't look so bad now that the socket has healed!

Pastor Don Kremer, thanks for your words of wisdom, encouragement and humorous tales. I think you said it best when you professed, "It's not what you know, but who you know!" On that note, my biggest expression of gratitude goes to Jesus Christ, for through Him, all things are possible.

—HEATHER MEHRA-PEDERSEN

INTRODUCTION

Yes! You're thinking about a new log home—one designed and built especially for you. There are so many options and opportunities, so many choices, and so much to think about! Where do you start—or, more appropriately, when did you start? You already know what you like. The magazines you buy, the pictures on your wall, the time you spend cooking, working, relaxing, or entertaining in your home are all part of your new design. Now write it down, then add in your aspirations, family plans, and hopes for tomorrow.

The home planning process is a gratifying personal journey, but you probably won't go it alone. Eventually, most homeowners will bring in architects, designers, or builders who will help them put foundations under their dreams. When that time comes, you want to be ready. Go with your sketches and lists, a box full of clippings, and a few good books under your arm. Although you may not be fully aware of all the limitations as they relate to your site or budget, at least you'll know what you want. And that, say the professionals, is a very good place to start.

The Log Home Plan Book is a beginning place. In compiling the homes and floor plans for this book, we invited log home professionals to send us some of their favorite designs. You won't find a book filled with black-and -white renderings. We give you beautiful color photographs of floor plans translated into actual log houses. Visit these plans and pictures and imagine how a daylight basement, a wide-open living area, or a second-floor loft might work for you. Picture how traffic flows through a home, note the placement of stairs, the relationship of a front entry to individual rooms, or how plumbing walls are shared to minimize costs.

Each plan is a resource—each photograph, a three-dimensional glimpse into personal lifestyles and home decor. Weaving it all together is valuable information, advice, and planning tips from the people who design and build log homes.

You may even find a plan that's almost perfect for you. But remember, no two families will ever be the same, nor will any two pieces of land be exactly alike. Your home might be a close second, but it should never be a carbon copy of someone else's dream. The plans in this book were customized to meet individual needs, and they can be customized for you. Most log home companies have in-house design services. In many cases those services are free if you purchase a log home package. In all cases, architects and designers can start with the plans you like best then one-up them for your family!

Each floor plan includes general room dimensions to help you visualize the size of important spaces. A home's size is also listed in terms of the number of square feet it contains. Be aware, however, that there are different ways to calculate this figure. For purposes of estimating the total cost of a log home package, measurements are taken from the outside of one wall to the outside of another. This number can be significantly different from measurements that calculate the actual living space contained within the walls (the difference can amount to several hundred square feet for large homes built with big logs). **In this book, the number of square feet is based on covered space contained inside the walls, and is not intended as a basis for calculating the finished cost of a home.**

As you study the plans and pictures, you might also notice occasional discrepancies. For instance, something may appear in a photograph that you can't identify in the floor plan. That's because, as blueprint walls are transformed into three-dimensional spaces, adjustments are often made. While major changes can be costly and difficult to execute during the building process, minor fine-tuning is possible and even called for. It's okay to fuss with nonbearing frame walls, move closets or add built-ins. Doors and window openings can usually be added or expanded, and porches and decks are easy add-ons. No doubt, you'll have your own ideas too.

In the end, changes, however possible, are best made on paper. Let time be the tool that builds your plan. Then let your plan be the tool that takes you home!

A WORD ABOUT LOG BUILDING COSTS

The other day we went out to buy a new car. We only do this about every six years, so we polished up on tire-kicking beforehand. We perused the newspapers, Internet, and other sources of information in order to prepare ourselves as best we could. Knowing exactly what we wanted, we sallied forth like Don Quixote, ready to slay our dragons. There was only one problem: the darn dragons wouldn't stand still. It seemed like there were so many variables that affected the selling price of the vehicle we couldn't tell whether this dealer or that one was giving us the better price. Between the different option packages (many of which we didn't even want), trade-in value of our existing vehicle, dealer preparation charges, etc., our heads were spinning. Finally, having spent a couple of weeks sorting things out, we did become the owners of a new car. Do we like the vehicle and trust the dealer who sold it to us? Is it what we wanted, needed, and could afford? Yes, yes, yes—but could we have gotten more for less somewhere else? Ah, heck. Who knows!

Wait a minute, you ask. What does buying a car have to do with building a log house? Unfortunately, a lot! Indeed, buying a house is even more complicated because there are more variables to contend with. And, like dragons, they won't stand still. Different companies package their products very differently, so you rarely find any two standard packages that make apple-to-apple comparisons a breeze. To complicate it further, labor and material costs for the same things can vary substantially from region to region.

In *The Log Home Plan Book,* it had originally been our intention to include price-per-square-foot costs for the log work associated with the homes in these pages. Upon further consideration, however, we decided that such figures might actually be a disservice to both our readers and the companies who did the work. Not only was it difficult to express costs in equitable 1999 dollar amounts, but those numbers did not encompass the same things. Additionally, in *The Log Home Plan Book,* we have generally listed the size of each home in terms of its interior living space. However, when a company bids on a log package, they commonly include space taken up by log or foundation walls. Thus, the overall size (and costs based on price per square foot) may be greater. Finally, the log package is just one component of the overall cost of a home.

Our advice: if you are a serious shopper and like something you see inside these pages, call the company to find out what you need to know to make meaningful comparisons between their home and someone else's. After all, it's fine to kick tires; you just don't want to end up kicking yourself!

CABINS, BUNGALOWS & HUMBLE ABODES

Move over, Abe Lincoln—America is moving in! Full of nostalgia and smitten with love, she knows of what dreams are made. There's no question that log-house architecture has grown up and, in doing so, staked claim to a place of respect and prominence in the contemporary house market. But who can forget those humble beginnings? Certainly not the myriad of families who yearn for a cabin—not a lodge. Such a retreat can shrink the whole wide world and speak rest to a weary soul. Some of these favorite small houses are year-round getaways; others are full-on family homes. Whether infinitely practical and budget-conscious, or "just right" in the scheme of great escapes and real-life make-believe, a scaled-down home might be just what you're looking for.

PHOTO: CINDY THIEDE

"There is pleasure in the pathless woods."
—LORD BYRON

CLOSE
TO
HOME

When you live so close to your vacation getaway, it's easy to cart seasonal gear back and forth. There isn't the urgency of having a place for everything. You can plan your cabin for living life in the moment. Simple! This basic design has everything a family of five needs. As for the essentials of summer, there's space for the hammock under the wraparound porch and a screened porch off the dining room.

PHOTOS: COURTESY OF MAPLE ISLAND LOG HOMES

R EMEMBER "COZY"? "It's what people seem to be missing in today's log homes," says Maple Island architect Gordon Hughes. Ironically, cozy has become a sort of luxury that isn't always practical in our primary residences where we have so much to do and so much to put away. Fortunately, the cottage at the lake can be different; in fact, sometimes it should be—has to be—if it's to succeed as a true place of refuge. Designed with a different set of priorities, this little cabin is only a half-hour's drive from its owner's Michigan home.

The living room is snug without feeling cramped. Cathedral ceilings open the space up, but, adds the architect, "not so much that you feel like you're sitting in a gymnasium!" The log walls were designed to accommodate as much as three inches of settling around the immovable stone chimney.

Shapely and bold, an open log staircase can be an expressive focal point in a home and make a small room feel bigger. If you're tight on space, however, consider framing in your stairs to create valuable storage underneath.

Cabin living is family living. A relaxed, intimate environment draws people close. When you're on vacation, there aren't those same expectations for personal space. When it comes to kids, half the fun is bunking together in the loft, and there always seems to be room up there for one more. This pop-out dormer is one of two added for light and character. Both are fully framed with logs. The wood windows are clad in forest-green pre-colored steel for durability and charm.

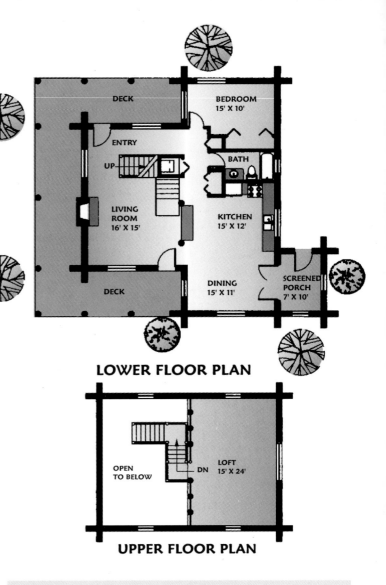

LOWER FLOOR PLAN

UPPER FLOOR PLAN

BUILDING A CASE FOR SMALL

Not only is the wood expensive, but log homes are notoriously labor-intensive to build and finish. Curvy walls meet in bumpy corners. Nothing is quite square, and there is a good deal more scribing, carving, and cajoling that come with the territory. That we save time and money by using less and doing less is obvious, but a well-built small home will also be less expensive to heat, cool, and maintain. Additionally, fewer square feet equate to lower annual property taxes, and a small home may enable you to spend more cash out-of-pocket, thus reducing or eliminating your need for a bank loan.

While architect Lester Wertheimer hadn't worked with logs before, he knew that every time you turn a corner, it will cost more time and money. So, why not start with a square? He began his design on a dinner napkin, taking into consideration the various constraints of their "smallish, uphill lot." He eventually devised a plan with the garage and utility room down below. The addition of a turret-like bay on the side of the house creates interesting interior spaces at half-levels. For instance, the front door opens into a stone-floored entry hall halfway between the garage and first floor. Another half level up are the first-floor living area and kitchen. Halfway up again is a little reading nook with Lester's desk and rocking chair. One more short flight up and they're in the bedroom.

PHOTOS: ELYSE LEWIN

ELYSE LEWIN WAS PHOTOGRAPHING *another* magnificent 10,000-square-foot house for a feature article in a prominent home magazine. In between the oohs and aahs, she and the enamored editor found themselves wondering: doesn't anybody ever build a beautiful small log house? The answer, it turned out, was "Yes, *we* can!" It just so happened that Elyse and her architect husband, Lester Wertheimer, were looking for such a home on Lake Tahoe's north shore. How about building one and having Lester design it? Of course, the magazine wanted to feature the finished home, so they would entice some of their advertisers into making special deals on appliances and furnishings. Alpine Log Homes embraced the opportunity to help with the log package. It wasn't long before two more brilliant local builders got into the act. With a full cast of committed professionals ready to go, the entire project took only six months from groundbreaking to picture hanging.

The tall, shapely fireplace tapers as it rises up to meet the ceiling. Height in combination with the taper creates what Lester calls a "forced perspective"—it makes the room feel taller and bigger than it actually is. The combination of stone and plaster feels a little bit European and cottagy, but really, says Lester, it's something that just happened. The stone recalls some of the local Tahoe architecture, and the couple liked the material, so they used it.

"Building small is easy! I like small spaces, but they demand high ceilings over the important gathering areas of your home. Low ceilings are nice when you want to feel hunkered in, but they'll just kill other spaces. You know, Frank Lloyd Wright used a lot of low ceilings—then again, he was a short guy."

—LESTER WERTHEIMER, ARCHITECT

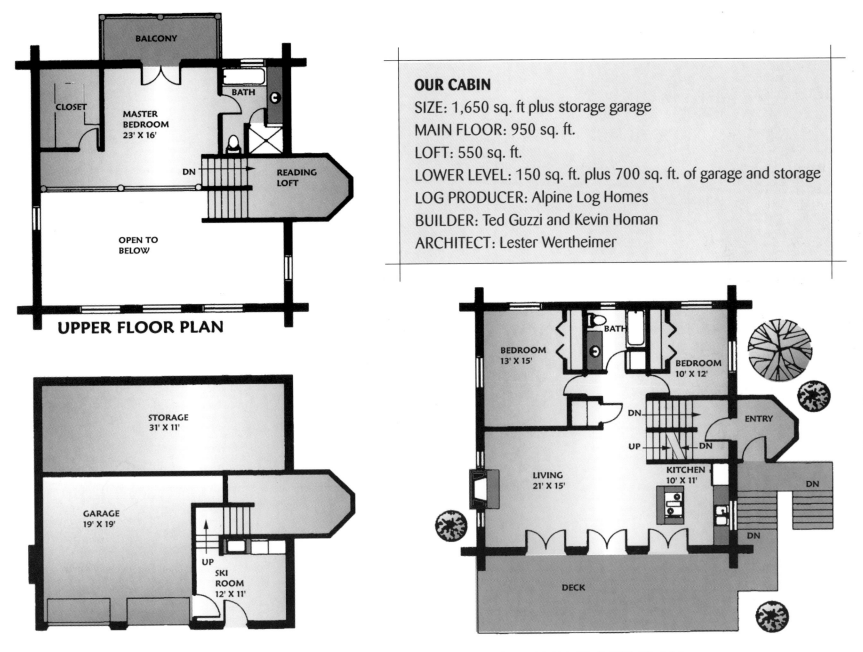

OUR CABIN
SIZE: 1,650 sq. ft plus storage garage
MAIN FLOOR: 950 sq. ft.
LOFT: 550 sq. ft.
LOWER LEVEL: 150 sq. ft. plus 700 sq. ft. of garage and storage
LOG PRODUCER: Alpine Log Homes
BUILDER: Ted Guzzi and Kevin Homan
ARCHITECT: Lester Wertheimer

UPPER FLOOR PLAN

LOWER FLOOR PLAN

MAIN FLOOR PLAN

Lester and Elyse had been to Switzerland, and while they weren't after a "cutesy Heidi thing," they liked the scale and proportion of what they had seen there. For instance, while large windows are nice because they grant more light and give the illusion of open space, divided light windows break things up and create a better scale. (Lester adds that there was no sense in using huge picture windows because there aren't any pictures out there—just houses). Lester also thought that horizontal logs showing between the glass doors and windows interrupted vertical continuity. His solution was to notch out the rectangular space in-between the doors and windows, then fit in boards painted a complementary blue-green. He added this feature both inside and out.

FILL 'ER UP!

"Chink" is the fill between horizontal logs. It seals up those notorious cracks that will leave log homes drafty and cold. In pioneer days, chink was whatever combination of mud, moss, sticks, stones, grass, or paper that a family could scrounge together. More sophisticated homes were sealed with mortar. Unfortunately, none of those materials remedied the problem very well. Over time, the logs would settle and the stuffing would fall out in fits and spurts. When synthetic flexible chinking arrived on the scene in the early 1980s, it quite literally saved the day! Because this new material was pliant and elastic, it didn't break apart with every shift and groan of a wall. Today chinking compounds come in a variety of colors, and the products just keep getting better. If you're shopping around, get references from people who have been in their homes for at least five years. Some compounds may be more elastic, adhere better than others, or be more durable. Be sure you ask for a warranty!

THE ROCKIN' DOUBLE D RANCH

Tucked away on a pristine lot in Big Sky, Montana, this mountain cabin started out as a spec house. The log shell of this handcrafted home was erected on the property in early November. While hardly the ideal time of year to start a home in snow country, the hardy father-and-two-son crew persevered by tenting the shell in a protective bubble of heavy-duty plastic called "rhino cloth." The home is built with standing-dead lodgepole pine and constructed with full round, chinked, saddle-notched logs.

PHOTOS: ROGER WADE

THE ROCKIN' DOUBLE D RANCH

SIZE: 1,580 sq. ft.
MAIN FLOOR: 1,050 sq. ft.
SECOND FLOOR: 530 sq. ft.
LOG PRODUCER: Frontier Homes, Inc.,
   (the Shoshone model)
DESIGNER: Hamilton Home Design
BUILDER: Elliott Iszler
INTERIOR DESIGNER: Carole Sisson

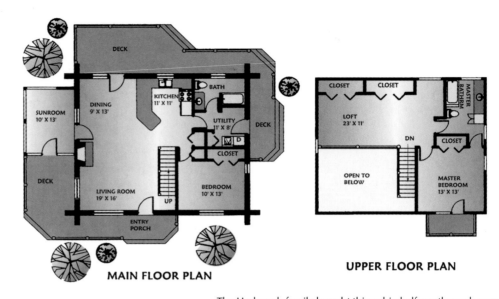

MAIN FLOOR PLAN

UPPER FLOOR PLAN

Do YOU REMEMBER those little cabins in the woods—so quaint they captured our hearts, so small we could actually afford them? Frontier Homes used to build more of them in the old days, and this home evolved with those quintessential memories in mind. The difference is, they wanted a full-season home that was as functional as it was delightful. Adequate storage, a small pantry, and combination laundry/mudroom were a must. So was a cathedral ceiling over the living room, second-floor loft, and stone hearth. The log package is simple and not too large. In keeping with the principles of economical design, the body of the house is square so there are only four log corners. The plumbing walls for both bathrooms and the kitchen are grouped together, and there are no hallways to take up extra room. Since the logs go only partway up into the second story, the gable ends are all framed, then finished outside with shake siding. The roof structure, however, is log. By adding on a sunroom, dormers, covered-entry porches, and a second-floor balcony at different eye-catching angles and heights, the boxy exterior is completely transformed!

The Harbaugh family bought this cabin halfway through construction—just in time to make a few significant changes. The most challenging was the addition of a second fireplace upstairs. Builder Elliott Iszler came through for the family by installing a ventless gas unit that didn't require the kind of complicated masonry stack that would have been out of the question. The firebox was framed in with wood and sided with lightweight synthetic stone. The gas line is hidden behind a chink joint!

ALL THE RIGHT QUESTIONS

Like cars, log home packages come in a variety of standards and options. Most all packages contain more than just the logs, but exactly *what* can vary so much that it makes comparison shopping a bit of a chore. While one company will provide logs for the walls, doors, and windows, another will include the roof, floors, stairs, and porches. Even the most complete packages, however, are a long way from the finished home. After all, there are still masonry work, floor coverings, appliances, countertops, built-ins, fixtures, and hardware, to name a significant few. It would be misleading for a company to give you a hands-down price for a finished home unless you have a complete description of materials right down to the nails. When selecting a log producer and a package, the best tack is to ask lots of questions—the kind of questions that good companies will be more than ready to answer:

• What is the species and size of your logs? • Are your logs graded? • Explain your building system and how the logs are cut and shaped when they arrive at my site. • What exactly does this package contain, and what will I still need for a complete weather-tight building? • Will the logs be predrilled for spikes, bolts, electrical wiring? • How was the wood dried and will there be problems when it settles? • Is the wood treated? Does it need to be in my area? • Are doors, windows, caulking, shingles, preservatives, etc., name brands I would recognize and trust? • Do the doors come pre-hung? Do the windows come with trim and screens? • What are the costs and conditions of delivery and erection of the shell? Will you be there? • What other costs should I plan for? Design? Blueprints? Manuals? Change orders, etc.? • Will my home meet local building codes? • What kind of warranty is included with the package? • How long have you been in business? Can I see some of your homes and meet previous clients?

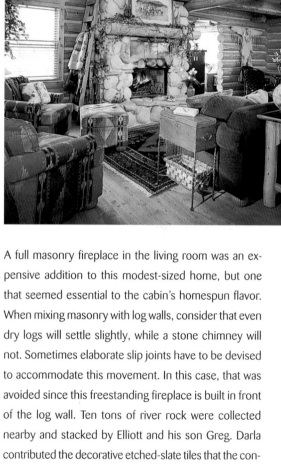

A full masonry fireplace in the living room was an expensive addition to this modest-sized home, but one that seemed essential to the cabin's homespun flavor. When mixing masonry with log walls, consider that even dry logs will settle slightly, while a stone chimney will not. Sometimes elaborate slip joints have to be devised to accommodate this movement. In this case, that was avoided since this freestanding fireplace is built in front of the log wall. Ten tons of river rock were collected nearby and stacked by Elliott and his son Greg. Darla contributed the decorative etched-slate tiles that the contractor inlaid into the stone just below the mantel.

This little kitchen is small but efficient. A breakfast bar extends up above the counter to make double use of the space. Since room was limited along the walls, a ventless Jenn-air cooktop and oven are reset into the extended counter. Colorful cabinetry is always successful in log homes since it contrasts so nicely with the wood.

THE
BRIDGER

Selected as one of *Log Home Living Magazine*'s top ten favorite plans in 1999, this milled-log home utilizes naturally cured, graded logs. Logs are examined for defects and randomly metered for moisture content by an independent contractor. The Bridger is built with nine-inch-diameter logs, but milled companies also offer home packages built with logs ranging from seven to twelve inches around. Generally, the larger the log, the more costly the shell.

PHOTOS: ROGER WADE

People sometimes wonder, "Won't we get tired of looking at logs?" "Never!" exclaims Thelma Yung, co-owner of Bridger Mountain Log Homes with her husband, Stan. "I can be gone for a week or a day, but when I come home, it's all brand new." Both their company and their log home are named for that rugged Montana explorer Jim Bridger and the Bridger Mountains to the east. The Hyalite Range, the Spanish Peaks, and the Horseshoe Hills lie south, west, and north. With 360 degrees of pure Montana range and wildness, the setting was made for this home that has become the Yungs' company showpiece.

People rarely enter their own homes by way of the front door. Think about where you park your car, then design a family entrance convenient to that area. Typically, you'll dump an armload of groceries first, so keeping the kitchen nearby has some obvious advantages. Laundry areas are often near the kitchen too, since you can peel the carrots, then load up the washer; put in the chicken and unload the dryer. This basic arrangement can be an important time-saver, especially for the working mom or dad.

THE BRIDGER
SIZE: 2,170 sq. ft.
FIRST FLOOR: 1,470 sq. ft.
SECOND FLOOR: 700 sq. ft.
DESIGNER AND LOG PRODUCER:
    Bridger Mountain Log Homes
BUILDER: Bridger Mountain Affiliate,
    Stan Yung Construction

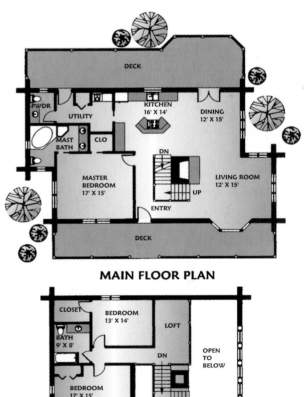

MAIN FLOOR PLAN

UPPER FLOOR PLAN

This zero-clearance fireplace is wood-framed and covered with synthetic stucco. The premixed material is more flexible than the real thing and less prone to cracking. It is also easier to work with and comes in a variety of colors. In decorating their log home, Thelma abandoned the Early American motif used in her former stick-built house in favor of something more ranch style. Wall hangings like the western blanket behind the fireplace are perfect enhancers for bumpy log walls. But, says Thelma, she didn't have any trouble hanging pictures either; because milled logs are so smooth and uniform, artwork sits nicely on the wall. Besides, it was liberating to pound nails willy-nilly into the logs and not worry about the kind of unsightly mistakes that would normally leave you patching holes in Sheetrock.

Logs, unlike milled lumber, are not always inspected and graded by independent professionals. Experienced builders know quality logs when they see them and cull out substandard material when constructing a home. Other companies, however, will actually subscribe to a grading service to emphasize their commitment to quality and reassure home buyers. Inspectors use special criteria to select logs that are rot-free, low in moisture content, and that won't be prone to conditions that will impact visual or structural integrity.

BUTT WHERE?

Milled-log-home producers typically utilize shorter logs ranging in length from ten to eighteen feet. This figure is determined in part by the equipment and the wood itself. There are machines that can handle much longer lengths, but, in most cases, a finished house will have some visible butt joints in the walls. For interior joints that can't be hidden by intersecting frame walls, kitchen counters or the like, a little extra TLC is called for on the job site. Companies like Bridger Mountain Log Homes pride themselves on producing walls that, when finished, are so finely sanded and polished that you have to be looking for the butt joints to notice them at all. When structural roof systems call for logs that are longer than milled members, companies can use the same hand-peeled wood available to handcrafters. In other cases, milled systems will incorporate additional trusses or reinforce their systems with steel.

Lofts tend to be signature pieces in log homes. They are a grand way to squeeze in niches and extra space without closing in a room. "We're rancher types," explains Thelma, "and I've always liked living space on one level. But," she adds, "our open loft makes the whole area look and feel so much bigger."

This cabin began as a square, but a four-gabled roof along with the interplay of timber, glass, and sculpted logs give this home an extraordinary geometry. Time will only improve the patina on this standing-seam copper roof that is, otherwise, nearly indestructible. Four-and-a-half-foot overhangs are smart design. Extended eves protect the logs from harsh sun and winter weather.

PHOTOS: CINDY THIEDE & JEFF WALLING

GIDEON'S CABIN

SIZE: 1,950 sq. ft.
MAIN FLOOR: 950 sq. ft.
LOFT: 450 sq. ft.
BASEMENT: 550 sq. ft. plus ample
    heated storage
LOG PRODUCER AND BUILDER:
    Bullock and Company Master Craftsmen
DESIGNER: Waltman & Company

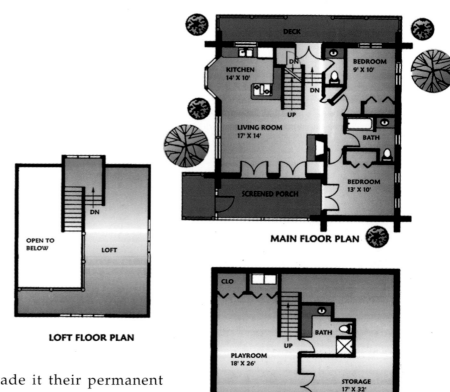

MAIN FLOOR PLAN

LOFT FLOOR PLAN

BASEMENT FLOOR PLAN

IN A GUEST HOUSE, you can sacrifice a little bit of practicality and still end up with a whole lot in return. Smaller closets, squandered space in the loft: tradeoffs perhaps, but not when it comes to artistic expression with wood. This gem-like cabin, with its multifaceted roof and magical palette of timber frame, birch bark, and patterned twig work is the result of a cooperative effort between artisans, master builders, and homeowners Liz and Allan Rosen-Ducat. And guess what? Minor impracticalities aside, the owners love this little house so much that when they made it their permanent home, they chose to add on rather than build a separate house off in their woods.

Since the gable ends were framed with timber and glass, the builders didn't want to introduce some other uninspired fill like clapboard siding or shakes. In the spirit of fun and regional Adirondack camp architecture, they chose to fill in the small triangular spaces under the eaves with birch bark. It was harvested locally and fastened with copper nails that won't bleed or rust away over time. Will it last? "It worked just fine on birch-bark canoes," says Tim, "and it's holding up well. I can't say we're surprised—just glad!"

"When you undertake a home project—no matter what your budget, you should think that your design is better than anything you've ever seen or done in that fashion before. Study the past, borrow from it, then beat it!"

—JOE WALTMAN, DESIGNER/BUILDER

MYTH: SETTLING IS BAD

Logs are alive. They live and breathe, shrink and settle. How much so, depends on things like the moisture content of the wood, the weight of the walls and structural members, and the home's environment. One thing's for sure—when the walls come down, so does everything else, including the posts, the stairs, and the plumbing stack! Competent log-home producers understand this, and settling, they say, should not be feared but understood. Once anticipated, there is not a single settling detail that can't be worked out.

From conception to completion, builder/designer Joe Waltman and master log craftsman Timothy Bullock brought different talents to the design table. Joe designed the home, then Tim interpreted that design to reflect the full potential of log and timber. They chose timber-frame construction for the second floor and roof because those milled members showcased the grain of the wood and provided striking contrast to the logs. "Originally," explained Tim, "we were just going to use pine timbers, but I discovered a supply of ash. It was just a wee bit more expensive and gave us the opportunity to build with a premium wood. It's prettier than oak or maple, straight grained, and strong."

Cathedral ceilings and a wide-open loft make this little house feel like a great big one! The Craftsman-style railings, woodwork, and cabinetry received the same amount of time-consuming care as the log and timberwork. A screened porch overlooking the lake was absolutely vital in this Maine environment where mosquitoes and black flies will carry off both kids and dogs! However, the screens are removable, so there's no sacrificing of sunshine in winter.

FLYING
HEART
RANCH

Art is a tree and shrub person. He loves to plant them, care for them, and watch them grow. He also loves to buy them and can't resist anything that smacks of a good deal. In our area, the fall is a favorite time of year to buy, since nurseries can't over-winter a lot of their stock and will offer it at substantial discounts. Aside from a tangle of aging cottonwoods near the highway, there wasn't a tree on our two-and-one-half-acre lot when we bought it. And while we did purchase some larger trees initially, our budget limited us to mostly small plantings. Within five years (about the time this picture was taken), our greens had added substantial value to the land and house. We ended up selling our homestead so we could build again, but you should see it now! Nearly a decade and a half later, the old place is as inviting as a park.

PHOTOS: CINDY THIEDE AND JONATHAN STOKE

FLYING HEART RANCH
SIZE: 2,200 sq. ft. plus a 450-sq.-ft.
   attached garage
MAIN FLOOR: 1,180 sq. ft.
SECOND FLOOR: 1,020 sq. ft.
DESIGNER, BUILDER, AND LOG
   PRODUCER: Art and Cindy
   Thiede, Woody's Log Homes

A WIDE-OPEN, FLAT, SCRUFFY, high-desert chunk of ground set alongside a major highway was not my idea of the perfect lot, but it did present the perfect opportunity to be creative. We had so many options! When Art and I built this home for our family in 1987, two of our most important goals were to buffer the home from highway noise and develop a landscaping plan that would both insulate and complement our little homestead in the making. While landscaping is often viewed as a nonessential, do-later item on the home builder's list, it remains the spit and polish that can give even the simplest home extraordinary appeal.

That certainty had us laying out temporary drip lines and planting trees before we'd even broken ground.

With new trees in the ground and growing, we finalized a site plan that would mute the roar of the highway beast behind us. We planned for three buildings—our house, the barn, and a separate father-in-law apartment for Art's elderly dad. We kept the house near the front of the lot and as far from the highway as possible. The barn went in behind the house to shield it from the busy thoroughfare. Our third building was placed lengthwise on the south side of the property between the house and barn. A row of new trees to the north would grow up to screen off the neighboring lot. The whole arrangement created a sort of large courtyard that was both private and secure.

The entire floor plan is laid out around this centrally placed stairway that helps divide the living space without closing it in. Foot traffic flows in a circular pattern around this pivotal element. A semiformal railing lends unexpected contrast between the blonde logs and the stairway that curves back to a small loft overhead. We added a gas fireplace in the step-down living room but installed a wood-burning stove in the family room. A gas forced-air furnace was our primary heat source, but we rarely used it since the wood stove provided more than enough heat to keep us warm.

"Learn from the mistakes of others. You can't live long enough to make them all yourself."

—Anonymous

This little sunroom was added on to dress up our economical but boxy design. Art cut costs by using standard patio replacement glass as opposed to custom-tempered glass units. The floor is simply slab-on-grade concrete girded into a square and painted dark to absorb heat. An exterior door leads to the backyard patio, so this room became the designated port of entry for kids with wet or muddy gear. French doors between the sunroom and house allowed us to close the room off in extreme weather or on cold cloudy days.

FRAME IT WITH TREES

It used to be that one could find idyllic property on which to perch a log home without a whole lot of difficulty and at a reasonable price. The problem now is that God isn't creating any more "purple mountain majesties" with babbling brooks and unbroken vistas. Instead, you're more likely to find (in your price range) an acre of sagebrush and a book of design restrictions. So, get creative! If there's one thing that will improve the value and enjoyment of your log home, it's the natural world that surrounds it. Don't fret over the cost of the granite countertops—eat off the plywood and plant some trees instead. Let the sun, water and nutrients in the soil work their magic. Put the frame around that picture.

—ART THIEDE,
AUTHOR AND BUILDER

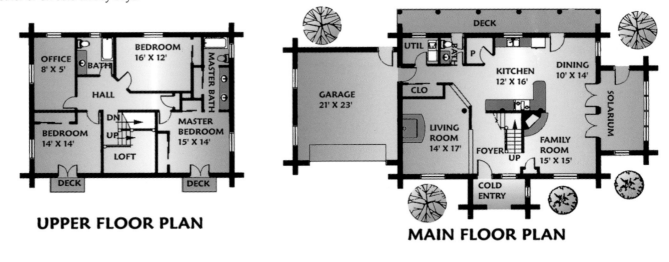

UPPER FLOOR PLAN

OFFICE 8' X 5'
BATH
BEDROOM 16' X 12'
MASTER BATH
HALL
BEDROOM 14' X 14'
DN
UP
MASTER BEDROOM 15' X 14'
LOFT
DECK
DECK

MAIN FLOOR PLAN

DECK
UTIL
BATH
P
GARAGE 21' X 23'
CLO
KITCHEN 12' X 16'
DINING 10' X 14'
LIVING ROOM 14' X 17'
FOYER
FAMILY ROOM 15' X 15'
SOLARIUM
UP
COLD ENTRY

In this age of mega-stores and ware-house shopping, a kitchen pantry can be a valuable asset in a home. Where else do you store two-foot-high cereal boxes and twenty rolls of paper towels?

Plumbing a log home demands extra thought and planning since you can't hide pipes in log walls. Nor can you hide them in the ceiling space between floors if the support system is built with exposed beams or logs overlaid with decking. The most common solution is to run plumbing pipes through interior framed walls. But even that isn't always an option in wide-open floor plans. If that's the case, you can gain flexibility by putting tubs or toilets on raised platforms, or build in chases like the one you see back in the corner of the dining room. That chase services the second-floor master bathroom. Of course, in cold-weather climates, you should also avoid running pipes along exterior walls because they are more susceptible to freezing. We just didn't seem to have a choice.

BEST LITTLE HOUSE

Resting like a nest amongst the birch and aspen trees, this hand-notched cabin was built with standing-dead lodge-pole pines (not a single living tree was sacrificed). Wedged between the river on one side and the majestic Teton mountain range on the other, this cabin is pure paradise.

PHOTOS: MARK BRYANT/COURTESY OF ALPINE LOG HOMES

BEST LITTLE HOUSE
SIZE: 1,178 sq. ft.
MAIN FLOOR: 968 sq. ft.
LOFT: 210 sq. ft.
DESIGNER AND LOG PRODUCER: Alpine Log Homes
BUILDER: Dembergh Construction

B UILT IN THE SHAPE OF A T, this modest cabin manages to do a lot with just a little. Open-beam ceilings, two master bedroom suites, nooks, big-windowed bays, and lots of decks earned it *Home Magazine's* "Best Little House" award in 1994. Throw in the sleeping loft with plenty of under-eaves storage, and you've got a vacation getaway that caters to a family of six without feeling too cramped!

Wraparound decks make this little cabin seem twice as big. All told, the decks encompass more than 1,000 square feet of seasonal living space. With four outside entrances, these exterior spaces are truly an integral part of the design. This window seat bay is one of two built into each bedroom. Both are framed additions finished off outside with log posts and siding to match the cabin.

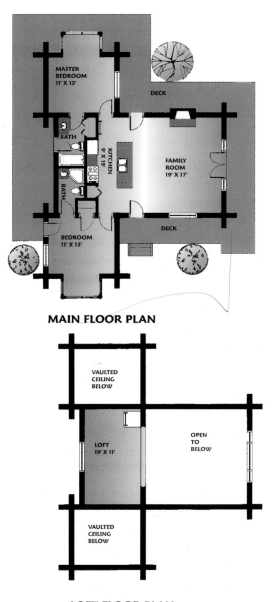

MAIN FLOOR PLAN

LOFT FLOOR PLAN

Anything this tiny retreat lacks in size is more than compensated for by the inclusion of full-log gable ends, massive double trusses, a masonry fireplace, cathedral ceilings, and large picture windows. Such are the things of which log cabin dreams are made! None of these features were inexpensive, but the practical scale of the house made them all possible.

OUT TO DRY

Trees are partly water. "Green" logs have a high moisture content, and will shrink substantially as they dry. Log-building companies know all about that, and they have devised various systems to stabilize their wood before building. The idea is to bring the moisture content of the wood into equilibrium with the environment (somewhere between 10 and 24 percent, depending on where you live). On one end of the spectrum are companies that prefer green logs. They expect shrinkage and build exceptionally crafted "shrink-to-fit" homes. Other companies carefully stack their logs and allow them to air-dry naturally over a six-to-eighteen-month period. To speed up the process, some producers kiln-dry their logs in large ovens. This more rapid, controlled drying process can take the moisture content of the wood down to around 15 percent. Kiln drying will also kill insects and larvae that may be in the wood. Finally, there are companies (primarily in the West) that use dead-standing trees killed naturally by fire or insects. Having dried out thoroughly over time, these logs tend to be quite stable. Which is best? Simple. Find a reputable company you trust with a product you like and ask them!

IT'S NOT BROKEN!

As moisture makes its way out of the wood, a single crack or check will often develop along the length of a log. These horizontal openings don't impair the structural integrity of the material, but builders are always careful to position logs in the wall so that significant checks are directed inside the house or, at least, out of weather's way. Occasional cracks that are set in a direction to catch and hold rain or melting snow should be sealed with caulk or chink.

The kitchen island doubles as a dining-room table in this compact design. Log siding on the island front fits well with the cabin decor. To the right, a log ladder leads to the sleeping loft—a special pleasure for any kid who can turn the upward climb into a pirate-ship adventure. A door behind the island on the left side of the kitchen leads to a bathroom shared with the living area and bedroom next door.

Window seats in the bedroom afford more than just a cozy nook to nap or read. Deep, under-seat drawers help offset the storage dilemma that can develop in a small home. Recessed cans in the bay ceiling provide a direct source of light for quiet-time activities like reading or needlework.

THE
PROW
STAR

Built with milled four-inch-thick cedar timbers, this solid-wood home is far more refined than most traditional log homes. Each timber is kiln-dried, then machine-edged with double tongues and grooves that lock together for an airtight fit. While four-inch walls have less thermal mass than the walls of homes built with larger logs, the same energy-efficiency principles apply. There is still enough mass for adequate insulation and heat retention, while the inability of air to escape through the walls keeps this home snug and warm—or cool, as the case may be!

PHOTOS: COURTESY OF LINDAL CEDAR HOMES

THE WOOD AT A TREE'S CORE is called heartwood. It is the most durable and decay-resistant part of the tree. Sapwood, on the other hand, makes up the outermost layers of a trunk. Fast-growing southern trees tend to have more sapwood than their slower-growing compatriots in the north. All trees produce natural toxins that protect them from insects and disease, but cedar, with its relatively high proportion of heartwood, has long been touted as particularly decay and pest resistant. Generally, that means that it is also more expensive. In the forest, the most plentiful trees are small ones, so cedar works well for companies who mill their wood. Designed and built by Lindal Cedar Homes, this prow-fronted home is built from western red cedar harvested near Vancouver, British Columbia.

THE PROW STAR
SIZE: 1,980 sq. ft. (does not include an optional basement)
MAIN FLOOR: 1,400 sq. ft.
LOFT: 580 sq. ft.
DESIGNER AND LOG PRODUCER:
    Lindal Cedar Homes

MY LOG'S BETTER THAN YOURS!

There are hundreds of log-building companies scattered throughout North America and about eighty commercial wood species available to build with. When choosing a particular species, a handcrafter might look for large-diameter trees with long straight trunks, few knots, and little taper. A manufacturer who machine-mills their logs might work with smaller, shorter trees. Both will want durable, decay-resistant wood, but by and large, they will use trees that are readily available and affordable. For one company, that might be a type of pine; for another, cedar; for yet another, oak, fir, hemlock, or spruce. More important than the wood species, say the experts, are the design and construction of the home. Even strong, decay-resistant wood will succumb to the elements in a home that is poorly designed or maintained.

Post-and-beam construction works well for large window walls because the vertical and horizontal members form a framework that stays rigid and supports critical loads. (On the other hand, large cutouts for windows in horizontal log walls may need additional beefing up, since the wall is weakened when large sections of wood are removed.) When designing with so much glass, it's important to match energy efficiency with your climate and to be aware of any building codes that might require the use of tempered or laminated glass. You may also want to consider low-e glass to improve performance and cut down on harmful UV rays that can fade your furniture.

Skylights like the ones over this dining-room table can bring coveted light inside any home. Different roof types dictate slightly different methods of installation, but properly done, skylights will be leak-proof. In cold-weather environments, skylights may be elevated a few inches above the roof to prevent the buildup of ice dams. Glass in a roof is generally engineered to hold loads up to seventy pounds per square foot. While snow will usually melt on skylights located over heated spaces, those in other areas (such as porch roofs over exterior decks) may need periodic clearing in winter.

"The most important step you can take to improve energy efficiency in a log home is to reduce air infiltration."
—LOG HOMES ILLUSTRATED

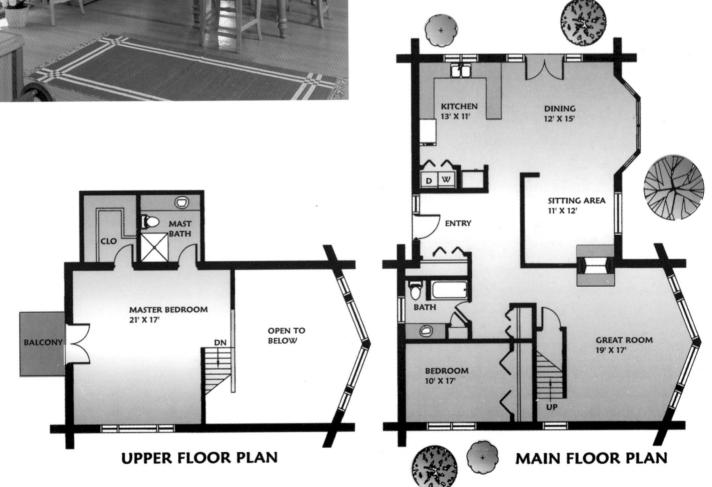

UPPER FLOOR PLAN

- MAST BATH
- CLO
- BALCONY
- MASTER BEDROOM 21' X 17'
- DN
- OPEN TO BELOW

MAIN FLOOR PLAN

- KITCHEN 13' X 11'
- DINING 12' X 15'
- D W
- SITTING AREA 11' X 12'
- ENTRY
- BATH
- GREAT ROOM 19' X 17'
- BEDROOM 10' X 17'
- UP

THE
NORTH
SLOPE

A large screened porch on the side of the house spills out onto the sculpted, multilevel deck. When the bugs die down in summer, large bifold doors fold out of the way, leaving one whole side of the porch wide open. The house started out small since Greg was a bachelor, but not the yard. In season, the whole outdoors becomes part of the living space. Today Greg has a wife and child, and they are adding on a substantial expansion. "We'll attach it 'gently,' " explains Greg's wife, Jamie. People suggested that they turn this portion of the house into separate guest quarters, but they said no. "This portion of the house is special and we want to live here!"

PHOTOS: CINDY THIEDE/JONATHAN STOKE

WHAT A SCORE! All the pieces of the ninety-year-old Scandinavian lap-notched cabin were stacked and ready for restoration. A foundation was constructed, and owner Greg Erickson along with Robert Chambers and Katherine Cartrette began the task of reassembling original cabin walls. Uh oh! Closer inspection revealed extensive rot concealed within the wood. There seemed little choice but to start over with new logs.

The floor plan remained the same along with all the door and window placements, but the home soon demanded a higher order of craftsmanship. What began as basic reconstruction rapidly evolved into something entirely different. "We treated the house like fine furniture but on a grand scale," says Robert. "It was a bit like building a live-in Scandinavian dovetailed chest."

Fresh-cut red pine logs were hewn flat and worked smooth. While the original cabin had simpler lap-notched corners, the new logs were precision fit with full dovetail notches. This traditional joint is more time-consuming to construct but keeps the logs firmly in place. Its design also helps to shed water away from the building. So precise are the notches that they look like wooden zippers. The roof is finished with multicolored slates, copper flashing, and heated coils that prevent snow buildup.

THE NORTH SLOPE

SIZE: 950 sq. ft. plus a basement with laundry facilities and storage

MAIN FLOOR: 550 sq. ft.

LOFT: 400 sq. ft.

LOG PRODUCER AND BUILDER: Robert W. Chambers with Owner Greg Erickson

ARCHITECT: Katherine Cartrette

"A plan is nothing, planning is everything."
—DWIGHT D. EISENHOWER

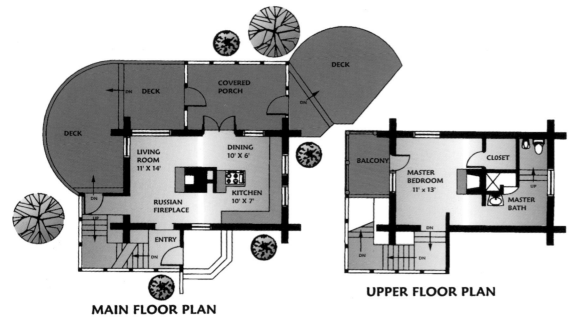

MAIN FLOOR PLAN

DECK

DECK

DN DECK

COVERED PORCH

DECK

DN

LIVING ROOM 11' X 14'

DINING 10' X 6'

KITCHEN 10' X 7'

RUSSIAN FIREPLACE

DN

UP

ENTRY

DN

UPPER FLOOR PLAN

BALCONY

MASTER BEDROOM 11' x 13'

CLOSET

MASTER BATH

UP

DN

DN

DN

SPECIALIZE

If your designer has not worked with logs, chances are your home will cost you more. Like other artisans, designers and architects get to know the ins and outs of the materials they work with most. Experience will mitigate problems before they arise. But it's not just about avoiding problems, emphasizes log home author, builder, and teacher Robert Chambers. What you might really miss out on are the opportunities! If someone has worked with and understands the medium, they will grasp the opportunity to enhance a room's ambience or create a special place. It might be nothing more than a well-placed post to lean on, but they'll know it when they see it!

Though less apparent from the front, this house is sited on solid bedrock and perched 180 feet above the Kinnickinnic River in western Wisconsin. Upstairs, the bedroom suite with its suspended walk-out balcony shares treetop space with the birds and squirrels. In polished contrast to the wall logs, roof trusses are framed with Douglas fir timbers salvaged from a grain elevator and warehouse.

Family Homes, Cottages & Moderate Residences

WHILE LOG CABINS still make the very best backwoods abodes, the buildings themselves have come in from the woods. Architects and builders have imbued them with the kind of sophistication that defies old-fashioned stereotypes but not old-fashioned charm. A better understanding of the wood itself along with the advent of synthetic chink, off-site building methods, and advanced joinery systems have made log homes a longed-for commodity in America, Europe and Japan—planned for and pursued by families sometimes for years it seems before becoming a reality. Why does it take so long? For one thing, custom log homes tend to be more expensive than comparable frame homes. For another, most are built in relatively rural settings for families

who have reached a more flexible station in life. Indeed, the people who build log homes tend to be slightly older and well established in their careers; often their children are nearly grown or gone. A log home may be something they've always wanted and finally the time was right.

The homes in this chapter round out the lives of different kinds of families. Versatile, stylish, and uniquely appointed, they demonstrate just how far log homes have come down that circuitous path of possibility!

PHOTO: CINDY THIEDE

"Plan ahead—It wasn't raining when Noah built the ark."
—JAMES B. CONANT

INDIAN
PEAK

"They don't call the Rocky Mountains rocky for nothing," says Tad Horning. Excavation often includes blasting to displace all the granite in the soil. The additional labor can add anywhere from $3,000 to $10,000 to the cost of a home project. Despite the extra expense, the Hornings firmly believe that you would be remiss not to take advantage of the inexpensive living space afforded by a walk-out basement on a gently sloping lot. They certainly incorporated one of their own, then faced it with synthetic stone. Real rock is cheap, says Tad. They probably could have picked it off their site for free. However, the labor and skill involved in laying it is another matter all together. Synthetic stone cost them more up front, but because it's lightweight and easily worked, they were able to set it themselves.

PHOTOS: BOB FRANZESE

Although the Hornings build log homes for a living, they spent more than a year designing their own. Their budget dictated a modest-sized house, so they employed the principles of open space to give people the illusion that the home is bigger than it is. There are few interior walls, and each room borrows space from the other. Alternately, individual living areas are separated and defined through structural details like the handcrafted log truss between the living and dining room and by different floor coverings. There is slate on the entry and kitchen floors, hickory in the dining area, and carpeting in the living room.

INDIAN PEAK
SIZE: 2,880 sq. ft.
MAIN FLOOR: 1,400 sq. ft.
UPPER FLOOR: 730 sq. ft.
BASEMENT: 750 sq. ft.
DESIGNER AND BUILDER: Occidental Log Homes, LLC
STAIRCASE: StairMeister Log Works

Tad Horning was in the sixth grade when he read an advertisement for a book on building log homes. That book led to others, and it wasn't long before he had read everything he could find that smacked of logs. By the age of thirteen (honest!), he knew that one day he would live in a log home. Tad says he met his future wife, Kimberly, in high school. They dated for awhile but came to a sort of crossroads. He really couldn't get too serious until he found out if she wanted to live in a log home too! That was over ten years ago, and today the couple owns Occidental Log Homes and a second company that specializes in handcrafted, spiral log staircases. ("Funny," says Tad, "back then, I didn't know people actually built log homes for a living.") Oh, and they do live in a log house—one they say so perfectly accents and complements their individual personalities that they believe they'll stay there forever.

Near the end of construction, the mason decided he had significantly underbid the stonework. Since there wasn't money to keep him nor time to find another, the Hornings decided to do the work themselves. They attended a two-hour seminar, purchased the cultured stone, then invited Kimberly's parents over night after night to help see them through. With scaffolding in place, Kimberly and Tad meticulously placed each rock. Now they believe their fireplace is one of the most beautiful aspects of their home, and, says Kimberly, "I know not a mason exists that would have cared as much as we did about the finished product."

"Spend the money on good plans and specifications provided by a design professional with log home experience. The money will come back to you four-fold."
—TAD HORNING, Occidental Log Homes

ELECTRIC BASEBOARDS?

Electric baseboard heat is quite inexpensive to install. And, although electric heat is usually more costly to operate, it makes good economic sense in certain situations. Consider, for instance, electric baseboard heat for seasonal summer homes or even winter cabins where most evenings are spent round the woodstove. You may still need supplemental heat, but if you rarely turn it on (or up), then electric heat will actually save you money. The same may hold true for upper floors filled with bedrooms. If you don't spend a lot of time there or prefer those areas to be cooler when you sleep, then think electric. By installing radiant or forced-air systems downstairs and electric baseboards upstairs, you can save a considerable amount of money on the cost of installation.

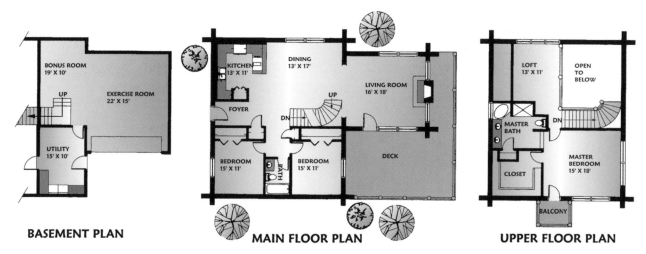

BASEMENT PLAN   MAIN FLOOR PLAN   UPPER FLOOR PLAN

BARGAIN BASEMENTS

Basements are the most cost-effective way to add square footage to a home. You can dig a deeper crawl space and kick up those foundation walls for about fifteen dollars a square foot. If you're tight on funds, the space can always be finished off later. Of course, a basement will still look and feel like a basement—unless you add light. If you plan on having bedrooms down below, building codes require you to install windows for emergency exit. Raising your first floor a few feet above grade is an easy way to address that need. *But*, if you have a gently sloping lot, good drainage, and accessibility, consider the ideal: a walk-out, daylight basement. A sloping lot will dictate more foundation regardless, so why not go the extra step and carve out that playroom, spacious laundry area, home gym, or guest rooms for the relations!

Kimberly wanted a full spiral staircase, but it wasn't practical in the given space. The sensible solution was a straight run, but that wasn't as pleasing. The answer came to them via this sweeping log stairway handcrafted by their company, StairMeister Log Works. The company designs and preassembles each set of stairs. Then, much like a handcrafted log-house package, the pieces are numbered and the stairs disassembled for shipping. Sometimes, says Tad, particularly intricate designs will be shipped mostly intact. Their company markets and sells their stairs all over the world.

COZY
ZEN

This roof is designed to shed snow off to the side of the house and away from entries and covered decks. Multiple gables were artfully added to break up the large run of roof from peak to eaves. Metal was chosen for its slick surface and fire-resistant qualities. There are two protected entrances to this home along with the covered decks in back. In winter, those outdoor living areas are important buffer zones from ever-growing walls of snow. A two-story enclosure around the front door offers extra relief from the weather, but it's not a cave. The round-top cutout above lets in the light and lends balance to fellow windows down the wall.

PHOTOS: BERYL MORRISON COURTESY OF OREGON LOG HOMES

WINTER IN BEAR VALLEY, California, means serious snowfall—twenty feet or more in a single season! That's good news if you relish all that white stuff and the recreational opportunities that come with it. This family's second home is built on a sloping site overlooking a lake. Summers are wonderful, but winter is pure magic. Once the snow flies, the road into the house closes, and the owners trade in their 4x4 for snowmobiles. The challenge of designing this four-season, winter-friendly cabin fell to architect Park Miller, who not only had to account for snow loads but for the potential of seismic activity as well.

COZY ZEN
SIZE: 2,800 sq. ft.
MAIN FLOOR: 1,600 sq. ft.
SECOND FLOOR: 650 sq. ft.
BASEMENT: 550 sq. ft.
LOG PRODUCER: Oregon Log
 Homes
ARCHITECT: Park Miller
BUILDER: Jere Foutz Construction

UPPER FLOOR PLAN

LOFT

DN

MASTER
BEDROOM
14' X 24'

OPEN TO
BELOW

CLOSET

MASTER
BATH

LIVING
17' X 19'

DECK

DINING
23' X 19'

UP

DN

BEDROOM
12' X 12'

RECREATION
ROOM
18' X 15'

CLO

DN

CLO

BATH

KITCHEN
14' X 14'

ENTRY

HALL

UP

UTILITY

BATH

BEDROOM
14' X 12'

PORCH

SKI
ROOM

BASEMENT FLOOR PLAN

MAIN FLOOR PLAN

HOW'S THE WEATHER?

Where you build your log house will have a big impact on *how* you build it. Different communities will mandate special structural requirements to make sure the home will weather heavy snowfall, moderate earthquakes, or gale-force winds. Minimum heating and cooling requirements are also addressed.

If you build in high mountain environments, plan for snow! For starters, you will need to beef up the roof to support the extra weight—in mountain resorts, 125 pounds per square foot is common, but that number has been known to go as high as 300 pounds per square foot in extreme climes. The design and pitch of the roof will be important too. Snow should slide straight off, but not into your entryway or in front of your garage doors. This is a particularly important consideration for metal roofs since they are supposed to shed snow. Consider raising your foundation above ground level to give your front door a head start in the race to stay above snow line. An impervious foundation faced with stone is a good alternative to other materials since prolonged exposure to moisture won't impact it visually or structurally.

Since this home sits on a hill that slopes down to the lakeside behind it, the architect set the house on top of a walk-out daylight basement. The front of the house is raised as well, with the first course of logs starting about four feet above grade. The roof is engineered to hold up to 300 pounds of snow per square foot, and the twelve-inch log walls are reinforced with steel from top to bottom to keep them from sloughing over in an earthquake. All the windows are double glazed (with two pieces of glass and an insulating air space in between). Because there is a popular snowmobile trail close by, the owners went to the added expense of using laminated "acoustic glass" in their master bedroom. While double glazing will also buffer noise, the added laminate in this special glass absorbs even more vibrations.

DOUBLE V RANCH

Kellie and Andy Vander Veur had been looking at big boats, not log houses. The cabin idea came up about the time they realized that a boat in Utah would only get used three or four months out of the year. So, unlike a lot of families, the Vander Veurs did not have a wish list or a notebook full of sketches. They did, however, have a trusted designer who was thrilled with the prospect of starting from scratch. Having spent time visiting the secluded five-acre site near Park City, Utah, Mark Bates designed a house with high glass in the living room. Perched on top of that is the master bedroom that manages to squeeze in the same gorgeous view through parallel windows in the gable end. A metal roof is the color of copper. It costs less than the real thing and, unlike copper, won't oxidize and change color over time.

PHOTOS: COURTESY OF ROCKY MOUNTAIN LOG HOMES

DOUBLE V RANCH

SIZE: 3,030 sq. ft. plus 529-sq.-ft. garage
MAIN FLOOR: 1,350 sq. ft.
SECOND FLOOR: 580 sq. ft.
BASEMENT: 1,100 sq. ft.
LOG HOME PRODUCER: Rocky Mountain
    Log Homes
DESIGNER: Bates Timber Design
INTERIOR DESIGNER: Colleen Horne,
    Andover West Interior Design

"Trust, but verify."

—OLD RUSSIAN PROVERB

DESIGNER MARK BATES has been creating log homes for more than twenty-five years, but "rustic" is not his thing. He prefers light colors and lots of glass. He seeks out uniformly sized and shaped milled logs, then has them hand-drawn for the craftsman touch. Light stains and chinking are also personal trademarks. As a firm believer in an airtight house, Mark says he chinks everything, including any significant checks or cracks in the exterior of the logs, around door and window openings, and along any other joint lines that might creak open over time. A well-sealed house will not just guard against those gentle breezes; it will also keep out flies and wasps that are literally drawn by the warmth of the wood.

Kellie and Andy admit that they were a bit undereducated when it came to log construction. Although they knew plenty about conventional methods of building, logs took them by surprise. Gleaning a better understanding of the nuances of the material and the cost of doing business took time. The couple's greatest challenge arrived when painters inadvertently used the wrong stain on the exterior of the house. It was so heavily pigmented that it obliterated the natural grain in the wood. Stripping off the color turned out to be a formidable task. By the time they arrived at the final finish, the house had been power stripped and sandblasted, nearly two years had passed, and more than one painting contractor had come and gone.

Something about our secluded site inspires people, says Kellie. Maybe it was the sense of peace or lack of distractions, but all the artisans who worked on the house went way beyond our expectations. One of the home's most original touches is the potpourri of pinecones and leaves hand-painted in the living room by local artist Emily Woodward Taylor. More of her artwork appears elsewhere in the house, including a wonderful aspen forest painted on the basement wall.

FOR THE LOVE OF LIGHT

Light-colored stains are showing up more often on the outsides and the insides of log homes. Gray weathering stains are often selected to make a home look old. Other times, the "light" look gives logs a clean, contemporary feel. There is no doubt that pickled or whitewashed interior walls brighten up a room. And designer Mark Bates believes that light colored homes are easier to maintain. The pigment in the stain gives added protection from ultraviolet radiation, but that's not all. With honey-colored logs, each new application of stain tends to darken the logs. Since some areas of a home will weather faster than others, partial applications of light colored stains are easier to blend. For instance, in Mark's own home, substantial roof overhangs protect all but the bottom four courses of logs. Those lower courses need attention more frequently than the rest of the home. He can re-brush those select areas without creating a visual break between new and old. That's not always the case with other finishes.

"My dad, my mom, my brother—we all cook!" says Kellie, so the kitchen had to work for a crowd. The open, well-laid-out design includes an extra-wide granite-topped island with a second sink for prepping vegetables. Knotty-pine cabinetry contrasts nicely with the light logs. They didn't cut corners, explained Kellie. Instead, they took an extra two years to finish off the house, so the costs were spread out over time.

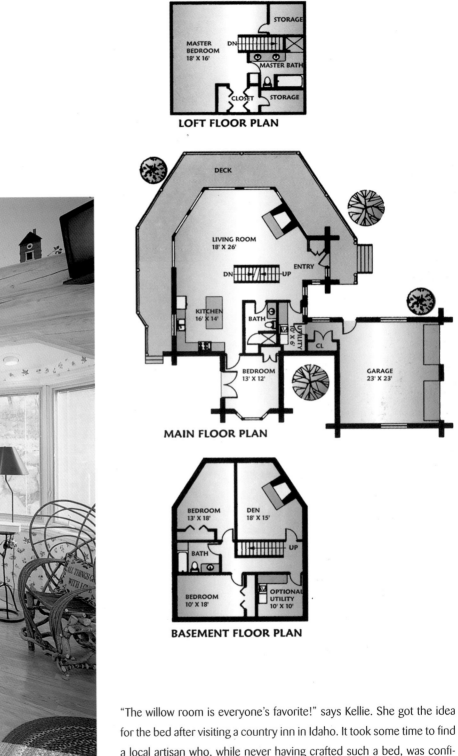

LOFT FLOOR PLAN

STORAGE

MASTER
BEDROOM
18' X 16'   DN

MASTER BATH

CLOSET   STORAGE

DECK

LIVING ROOM
18' X 26'

DN   ENTRY   UP

KITCHEN
16' X 14'

BATH

UTILITY
10' X 6'

CL

BEDROOM
13' X 12'

GARAGE
23' X 23'

MAIN FLOOR PLAN

BEDROOM
13' X 18'   DEN
18' X 15'

BATH   UP

BEDROOM
10' X 18'   OPTIONAL
UTILITY
10' X 10'

BASEMENT FLOOR PLAN

"The willow room is everyone's favorite!" says Kellie. She got the idea for the bed after visiting a country inn in Idaho. It took some time to find a local artisan who, while never having crafted such a bed, was confident he could. More of Emily's artwork in the gable end complements the wallpaper used below in the pop-out bay. The lampshade next to the bed is also hand painted with a matching design.

When it came down to designing the house, Mike quips that he was in charge of the garage, septic system and the bills, while Sandy staked claim to just about everything else! In reality, Sandy worked hand in hand with Custom Log Homes designer Ronaele Mello, laying out the open floor plan and developing the face of the home. Arched windows in the front match the curve of the entry door. Pop-out bay windows on the side of the house cost more, but they bring so much extra light into the kitchen that it was well worth it, says Sandy. On the inside, the kitchen sink and extra-deep counter spill into one of those bays, creating a wonderful, nurturing spot for indoor plants and garden herbs.

PHOTOS: CINDY THIEDE AND JONATHAN STOKE

RETIREMENT FOR Mike and Sandy Killion did not so much signal a change of pace as it did a change of place—from sailboats and the southern California seaside to the ski slopes of central Idaho. Along with that came the log home that they had been imagining and musing over for more than two years.

The red, round-top door is a partial copycat from the Killion's last home, a cottage built in 1928—"by elves!" adds Mike. "You had to stoop down to get through the door." Local craftsman Mark Hankinson built this version taller and added a peephole. As work on the house progressed, the Killions created a cold entry inside their home by adding glass doors to insulate the foyer from the rest of the living space. Though not included in their working drawings, doors were an easy add-on that increased the energy efficiency of their house.

MAIN FLOOR PLAN

- CLOSET
- BATH
- GARAGE 28' X 24'
- STUDY 15' X 17'
- 1/2 BATH
- UTILITY
- UP
- GREAT ROOM 20' X 15'
- ENTRY
- KITCHEN 15' X 18'
- DINING 12' X 22'

UPPER FLOOR PLAN

- BALCONY
- MASTER BEDROOM 18' X 19'
- BATH
- BEDROOM 10' X 19'
- CLOSET
- DN

HANDS-ON IN IDAHO
SIZE: 2,250 plus a 672-sq. ft attached garage
MAIN FLOOR: 1,600 sq. ft. plus 672 sq. ft. in garage
UPPER FLOOR: 650 sq. ft.
LOG PRODUCER: Custom Log Homes
DESIGNER: Ronaele Mello, Custom Log Homes
BUILDER: Burr Smith and the owners

Maybe it was all those days spent sailing at sea, but Sandy likes wide-open spaces and shuns interior doors. Even the master bedroom is partially open to the stairs and living area below. "Privacy is just not an issue," says Sandy, "since most of the time it's just the two of us." A fireplace upstairs shares a chimney chase with two more back-to-back hearths downstairs in the living room and study. All three units are Rumsford designs with high angled backs that help direct more heat into each room. A small, high-cut window on the left-hand wall brings added light into the bathroom.

The kitchen is the heart of this home, where at one time or another you'll find the island buried under the workings of a sumptuous meal, piles of fabric, needles and thread, or annual tax preparations. It needed to be big to accommodate Mike and Sandy's lifestyle, but it also needed to be organized to accommodate all of Sandy's kitchen tools and accessories. Once Sandy and Custom's design staff had good working floor plans of their home (and before they broke ground), Sandy hired an interior designer to look them over for about an hour (all her budget would allow). The designer noticed that the triangular kitchen island seemed too small for the space. Her observation led to this much larger, rectangular island that incorporated more interior storage space and ample under-counter shelves for cookbooks. It also includes built-in display racks for dishes on one end and spices on the other. This single improvement changed the workability and subsequent enjoyment of the entire kitchen.

Since they are hands-on people, they wanted to be involved in every stage of the design and building process. It was important to find a building company that saw this as a good thing.

Mike donned his tool bag and worked alongside the crew every day. As a retired electrical contractor, he also designed the lighting system for their home. Since light is absorbed by wood, it takes more of it to achieve the same level of illumination in a log house as in a comparable home with light colored frame walls. Vaulted ceilings also pose a challenge since they add so much volume to a room. Mike found track lighting to be the most versatile and cost-effective, particularly in high-ceiling areas where recessed cans were less practical.

LIGHTING YOUR LOGS

A lighting scheme for any home requires foresight and planning, but that goes triple for logs! You can't hide a wire in a solid log wall unless you've pre-drilled the holes to accommodate it. Though last-minute additions may be possible in miscellaneous stud walls, or by hiding wires behind chinking lines, the time to finalize your exterior and interior lighting plan is before your log walls go up—and most certainly before the roof goes on. When it comes to pre-wiring, "less is not more," say the experts. It's okay to plan for more than you need. When it comes right down to it, you don't have to install every light. You can also incorporate dimmer switches, use lower watt bulbs, and, of course, turn the lights off when you leave a room!

The stairway design was inspired by a picture in *Architectural Digest*, but it adds to the Southwest flavor sprinkled here and there throughout the house. Log ends protruding through the stucco are not structural. The short sections were added later for show.

Though the Spikers had originally set their sights on a one-story home, they learned that it was far more cost effective to build up than out. They also had a steeply graded lot that lent itself to the ideal: a daylight walk-out basement. With older children, a three-level house enabled the perfect separation of space. The kids' rooms (along with the TV and their personal stereos) are down below. Since Wes enjoys listening to music while he reads, he spends leisure time in the main-floor living area. Chris likes to read in total peace and quiet, so the third-floor master bedroom suite is her getaway spot. The family chose to combine stucco with their logs because they wanted to keep things light, and, says Chris, "We'd really never seen it done before."

PHOTOS: COURTESY OF ROCKY MOUNTAIN LOG HOMES

FOR ABOUT SEVEN YEARS, Chris and Wes Spiker had thrown their clipped home ideas into the proverbial dream box. "We started even before we knew we wanted logs," says Chris. "But eventually, everything we liked just pointed in that direction." They purchased land, made sketches, and met with designers. They actually went through two architects and two sets of renderings that didn't work out. Chris says, "One was just too big and the other was a one-level ranch house with $50,000 dollars worth of windows!" In the end, however, that extra effort helped get them where they needed to be. When Randy Hone came through with the third and final design, everything fell neatly into place—for the family, their budget, and the site.

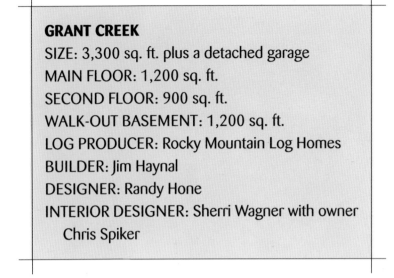

GRANT CREEK
SIZE: 3,300 sq. ft. plus a detached garage
MAIN FLOOR: 1,200 sq. ft.
SECOND FLOOR: 900 sq. ft.
WALK-OUT BASEMENT: 1,200 sq. ft.
LOG PRODUCER: Rocky Mountain Log Homes
BUILDER: Jim Haynal
DESIGNER: Randy Hone
INTERIOR DESIGNER: Sherri Wagner with owner
  Chris Spiker

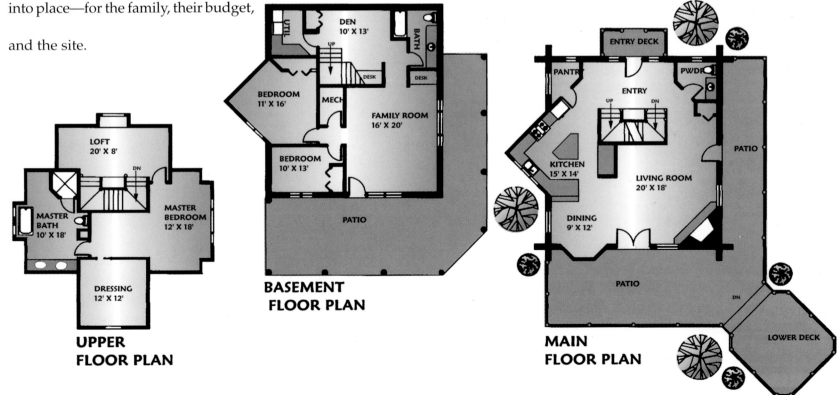

UPPER FLOOR PLAN

BASEMENT FLOOR PLAN

MAIN FLOOR PLAN

This house includes four pop-out frame and stucco dormers juxtaposed to the logs in a particularly unique way. Behind the bed in the master suite, a bay extends about two and a half feet beyond the exterior log wall. Meanwhile, those wall logs are trimmed away in a triangular pattern that highlights the specially made window and gives added depth and dimension to the space.

An antique claw-foot tub rests on a decorative tile pad in the master bath. With the exception of this space and small areas around the toilet and shower, everything else upstairs is carpeted. The cutout in the log wall above the tub frames the pop-out window like a work of art.

METALLIC BOND

What lasts longer than composition shingles, requires far less maintenance than cedar shakes, and won't catch fire when your chimney starts spewing briquettes? Why, a metal roof of course! Although metal may not come immediately to mind as the traditional log home roof topper, more and more families are selecting this material for their homes. They do tend to cost more, but if you like the aesthetic, the benefits are worth it. Metal roofs are also lightweight and adaptable to most roof systems. They shed ice and snow, help keep a home cooler in summer by reflecting heat rather than absorbing it, come in a rich variety of styles and colors, offer excellent wind resistance, and can be warranted to last up to fifty years!

Some of the kitchen walls are frame-built and finished inside with Sheetrock. The owners chose this option to add white space and eliminate bulky log corners inside where the kitchen wall intersects with the dining area. On the outside of the home, these framed sections are sided over with half-logs to match the rest of the building.

A river-rock fireplace in the living room was on the list of "must haves." However, the family did not want a fireplace in their basement. This posed a problem since river rock is extremely heavy, and such a structure on the second floor would technically need to be supported by a solid masonry foundation anchored at ground level. They solved their dilemma by framing in the fireplace surround and facing it with cultured stone. This lightweight material is a convincing counterfeit that comes in a variety of styles and colors and goes up in half the time. Forgoing a two-story, full-masonry structure saved them an estimated $15,000, says Chris, and nobody can tell the difference!

Like so many other families, Terry and Sonja picked a standard company plan as their starting point, then adapted it to suit their needs and lifestyle. Hearthstone was happy to comply, and there was no additional fee for this service. With the shell up, the couple did 95 percent of the finish work themselves, including the electrical, plumbing, chinking, and finished roof (to name just a few). All told, the house includes around 75 tons of stone, 162,000 pounds of logs, and 2 tons of chinking. There's no doubt that it took more time to build than a conventional home, but they estimate a 50-percent cost savings along the way. "Even more importantly," says Sonja, "this log home represents our commitment to traditional values." And they take pride in the knowledge that it will endure for countless generations to come.

PHOTOS: CINDY THIEDE AND JEFF WALLING

AN OWNER-BUILDER'S BEST
SIZE: 2,800 sq. ft. plus a basement garage with laundry area
MAIN FLOOR: 2,000 sq. ft.
SECOND FLOOR: 800 sq. ft.
LOG PRODUCER AND HOUSE PLANS: Hearthstone

LOG HOMES HAVE LONG BEEN a symbol of America's pioneering spirit. They root us to our past in a proud sort of way. Even today (or especially today) the notion that someone could harvest their own trees then shape them into a home with the simplest of tools is hard to resist. The fact that most modern-day log home companies pre-shape their logs, label the pieces, then ship entire home packages off to the buyer's site for step-by-step reassembly makes log homes a shoe-in for aspiring owner-builders. While no one should rush into such a project without careful thought, serious planning, and an unwavering commitment to their task, myriads of families do succeed in building, at least in part, their very own log homes.

Terry and Sonja Rosenberger purchased their log house package from a company that special-

A working waterwheel was always on Terry and Sonja's someday list, though it was never in the budget. From Terry's way of thinking, that just meant he'd have to build it himself. Working by trial and error from his own design, he pieced the wheel together in less than two weeks. As it turns out, the more difficult dilemma was getting enough water to the mill for proper operation. That led to the creation of two small ponds and a creek, along with extensive landscaping that ultimately included a covered bridge!

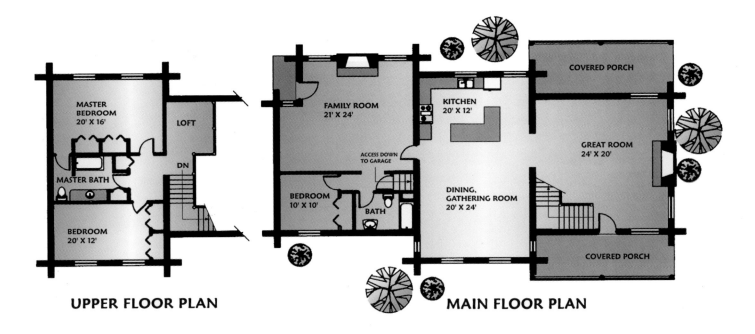

UPPER FLOOR PLAN

MASTER
BEDROOM
20' X 16'

LOFT

MASTER BATH

DN

BEDROOM
20' X 12'

MAIN FLOOR PLAN

FAMILY ROOM
21' X 24'

KITCHEN
20' X 12'

COVERED PORCH

GREAT ROOM
24' X 20'

ACCESS DOWN
TO GARAGE

BEDROOM
10' X 10'

BATH

DINING,
GATHERING ROOM
20' X 24'

COVERED PORCH

izes in traditional hewn-log construction with dovetail joinery. In this case, Hearthstone precut and engineered each log at their company mill, then shipped the package to the Rosenbergers' site along with the crew to help erect it. The shell was up in a matter of days, then the crew was gone. It was wet, sloppy, and cold that spring, and Sonja recalls thinking that the shell looked more like a cattle corral than a house. At first, she wondered if they'd made a mistake, but the die was cast and they never looked back.

Covered porches with protected entries are included on each side of the house. This back porch accesses the kitchen and is roomy enough to accommodate comfortable porch furniture. The gazebo in the distance is another owner-built signature piece that gives this home an extraordinary presence.

Sonja never wanted a lodgy home with trophies on the wall. Instead, she was after the country feel that she communicates so successfully through her furnishings. Like the home itself, many of the pieces were hand-made by the family for fun and as gifts for one another. Terry and their son craft furniture as a hobby, while Sonja and her daughter are expert seamstresses who have fashioned enough country collectibles to fill a gift shop.

"You can't have everything.

Where would you put it?"

—STEVEN WRIGHT

HANDMADE OR PRECISION CUT?

A log is a log is a log—NOT! When it comes to choosing a log style, you have dozens of choices. The most basic, however, begins with your decision to build either a handcrafted home or a manufactured one. If you don't already know exactly what you want, then here are some things to think about. Manufacturers use machine-peeled and notched logs. Each log is precision cut and short sections of log can be pieced together to span a wall. Machine-milled companies are often able to utilize smaller logs, and the finish appearance of a home is more uniform and refined. The pieces of a milled-log package will be labeled and numbered, but the home will not be prebuilt before arriving at its final destination.

When purchasing a log home package, you can hire a company crew to take the house to varying stages of completion. In this case, Hearth-stone only erected the basic shell and set the skeletal framework for the roof. Everything else was left up to the Rosenbergers. In the case of the stairs and loft, the company supplied the raw materials, and Terry did the rest.

THE
GLENWOOD

Most company-produced log homes (whether custom designs or not) are sold as packages that come in varying degrees of completeness and price. While one package might include only logs for the walls, others will provide everything necessary to rough in a house, from the doors and windows to a dried-in roof. In many cases, owners purchase a log shell, then save money by shopping around for big-ticket items like doors and windows. However, because of the preassembled and precut nature of these walls, Town & Country considers that their own company doors and windows play an integral part in the successful functioning of the home. In fact, a home package provided by this company typically includes everything needed to finish the home both inside and out, with the exception of mechanicals, masonry, finished flooring, and cabinetry.

PHOTOS: BRAD SIMMONS, COURTESY OF TOWN & COUNTRY CEDAR HOMES

THE GLENWOOD

SIZE: 2,400 sq. ft. plus attached
    garage with 400-sq.-ft. bonus
    room up above
MAIN FLOOR: 1,600 sq. ft.
SECOND FLOOR: 800 sq. ft.
DESIGNER AND LOG PRODUCER:
    Town & Country Cedar Homes
INTERIOR DESIGNER: The Quiet
    Moose/Compass Interiors

WINDOWS TO THE WORLD

Next to logs, your second-biggest home expenditure will often be for windows. Windows let in natural light, ventilating air, solar gain, and the view while keeping out everything from the wind and weather to noise and bugs. In log homes, efficient, well-placed windows completely rescue interiors from the dark and dreary nemesis of old. They also shape a home's personality. Various types of glass are designed to meet different needs in a home. Some are super-insulated; others are shatterproof and heat resistant. Sometimes glass is treated to help reduce heat loss or gain or to filter out some of the ultraviolet radiation that will fade carpets and furniture. Building codes also mandate the use of different types of glass, such as shatter-proof window near stairs or in patio doors. When planning your home, consider the exposure of each elevation and the way you live in various spaces, then mix and match glass types to maximize comfort and efficiency in every room!

GREEN TRIM ACCENTUATES the dramatic geometric display of glass in this Town & Country Cedar Home. There is actually more window than wall—a design feat that works handily with this manufacturer's special post-and-sill building system. The walls come in preassembled panels framed with vertical boards and filled with rigid sheets of foam insulation. Each panel is sided with half-round white cedar logs. With panelized walls, there is no such thing as settling. The panels arrive at the building site in four-to-six-foot sections with door and window cutouts already made. Pieced together like a puzzle, the home goes up very quickly.

PATIENCE, PATIENCE

Don't be so quick to cover those windows. Given time and occupancy, you will identify the practical requirements regarding what you use in respect to privacy, sunlight, and aesthetics. Not jumping the gun will enable you to choose accordingly and accurately.

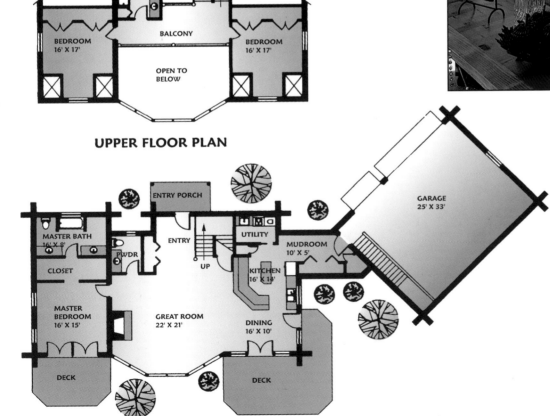

UPPER FLOOR PLAN

BATH

BEDROOM
16' X 17'

BALCONY

BEDROOM
16' X 17'

OPEN TO BELOW

ENTRY PORCH

GARAGE
25' X 33'

MASTER BATH
16' X 8'

ENTRY

UTILITY

PWDR

MUDROOM
10' X 5'

CLOSET

UP

KITCHEN
16' X 14'

MASTER BEDROOM
16' X 15'

GREAT ROOM
22' X 21'

DINING
16' X 10'

DECK

DECK

Set on a golf course in Petoskey, Michigan, this home received the National Association of Homebuilders 1998 award for "Outstanding Model of the Year." Designed with the aging parents of a well-connected but far-flung family in mind, this retreat is meant to be both a retirement home and a family center.

Facing photo: From the exterior, this home looks very much like it's built with full-round logs. It's not, but the illusion is realized through the addition of round log ends at the corners.

SAPPHIRE

"We're empty nesters," explain the Morelands. "Since the kids are grown, this home is smaller than our last." The guest bedrooms are upstairs, and the master bedroom and bath are on the main floor. Unless they have company, there's no need to go upstairs at all except to clean. A belvedere on the rooftop was Mark's real inspiration. Reminiscent of the old cupolas atop historic barns, it was added for it's architectural appeal. But Mark says it's also functional and fun. You can climb up there on an old ship's ladder and hang out. When you open the windows, you create a chimney effect that pulls hot air out of the house.

PHOTOS: COURTESY OF ROCKY MOUNTAIN LOG HOMES

B̲UILD THE EXACT SAME HOUSE TWICE? After twenty-five years, it hasn't happened yet, says Mark Moreland, vice president of Rocky Mountain Log Homes. Although people may start with a standard company plan, they will always change something. "And so they should!" is the general cry heard round the industry. With today's computer-aided design (CAD) systems, customizing a company plan is expected, and it's easy. Clients can sit down in front of the screen with a designer or send thoughts and scratchings back and forth via fax or the Internet. With CAD, it doesn't take more than a few keystrokes to enlarge the master bedroom, move the kitchen, or attach the garage. But what about Mark's own home? Mark says that having seen so many different log homes over the years, he and his wife wanted to do something out of the ordinary. They used in-house designers and the CAD system to formulate their plan from the conception stage on up. But, adds Mark, "I'm not sure any of our ideas were truly original." Perhaps not, but good design is borrowed, then adapted and custom fit to meet the needs of one particular family: in other words, a perfect fit. And that is unique!

SAPPHIRE
SIZE: 2,500 sq. ft. plus 475 sq. ft of attached garage
MAIN FLOOR: 1,800 sq. ft.
SECOND FLOOR: 700 sq. ft.
DESIGNER/BUILDER: Pioneer Log Homes
INTERIOR DESIGNER: Susie Moreland/By Design Interiors

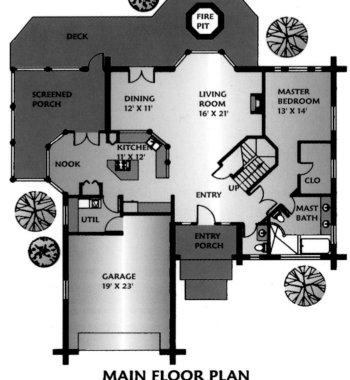

UPPER FLOOR PLAN

MAIN FLOOR PLAN

An arched doorway and open-beam ceiling carry over from the bedroom into this master bath. Fluorescent lighting is tucked away in sculpted soffits above the tub. For warmer light with better color rendering in this area, decorator Suzie Moreland recommends the use of full-spectrum fluorescent bulbs. The walk-in shower built with glass blocks is clean and contemporary. There are a lot of hard surfaces in a bathroom, so Roman shades were used over the windows for their added warmth and texture. This same fabric is used again in the bedroom.

MORE ROOM FOR LESS:

If you've got a framed roof instead of a trussed one, think about turning your attic into living space. Build in dormers to increase your headroom, and still save money over the cost of adding a full second story.

After too many years of golden brown logs, the Morelands wanted something different—and more contemporary. They chose light colored logs and a standing-seam metal roof. For practical purposes, the house includes an attached double-car garage, but personally, Mark is more interested in the little building next door. Apart from another storage bay, there is a "hobby" studio upstairs, where he can lay out tools and supplies and leave them for days on end. It's his space!

THANKS TO ALL MY FANS!

Combine open windows with a ceiling fan and you can drop the room temperature by four degrees without an air-conditioner. Not only does a fan pull cooler air up from below, but it also exhausts heat build-up in your home.

Susie, the Morelands' sister-in-law and interior designer, calls the decor "colonial goes west." Though the log portion of the house feels contemporary, Mark and Pat have more traditional tastes in furniture. "The dilemma in great rooms," explains Suzie, "is finding a successful arrangement between the view, fireplace, furniture, and entertainment center." In this home, the television and stereo share niches in raised-panel cabinetry surrounding the fireplace. As long as your television set isn't gigantic, this shared space seems to be a nice compromise. When planning your log home, Mark advises you to plan for entertainment systems in more than one area of the house. Run your wires upstairs and down. Then, if you find you don't need speakers in every location, you don't have to hook them up.

A BRIGHT IDEA

Fluorescent tubes are an extremely efficient form of lighting since they generate almost no heat and last thousands of hours longer than tungsten lamps. They produce a flat even light that is ideal for work spaces, so you'll find them used in utility areas, home offices, kitchens, and baths. The downside is that fluorescent light tends to be cool, harsh, and less flattering to flesh or earth tones. Furthermore, the shape of the tubes limits fixture selection. Dimmers are also expensive and harder to come by. Warmer fluorescent lighting is available, however, so if you go this route, check them out!

POETRY IN WOOD

Architect Richard Fisher was not a log-home veteran when he set out to design this home. Knowing that logs presented different challenges and opportunities from conventional architecture, he chose to work closely with Jack McNamara, an experienced log building contractor. Along with the owner, they spent time poring over ideas, revisiting pages from various books, and inventing the theme that would be carried throughout the house. Richard likens the design that evolved to a "mountain bungalow." The distinctive shake roof with its hips and dormers calls to mind Adirondack great camps, national-park lodges, and even Japanese pagodas. Fisher chose a cold-roof design engineered to hold the heavy snowfall characteristic of this mountain environment.

PHOTOS: CINDY THIEDE AND JONATHAN STOKE

POETRY IN WOOD

SIZE: 3,100 sq. ft. plus optional basement
MAIN FLOOR: 1,800 sq. ft.
SECOND FLOOR: 1,300 sq. ft.
LOG PRODUCER: Art Thiede and Norin Borke
BUILDER: Jack McNamara
ARCHITECT: Richard A. Fisher, AIA
INTERIOR DESIGNER: Susan Niven

AROUND THE TURN of the twentieth century, as the developing world embraced gadgetry and machines, certain architects and builders rose up in defense of handcrafted art. Young American architects like Frank Lloyd Wright, Gustav Stickley, and the Greene brothers eventually rose to fame with warm, livable house designs that have since become synonymous with the Arts & Crafts movement. In many ways, America's return to log home living represents similar desires to stay close to nature.

Both rustic and sophisticated, this log house incorporates the feel of a mountain lodge with the warmth and craftsmanship inherent in those early Craftsman-style bungalows. Logs coupled with hip roofs, shingled dormers, and transom-style windows are telltale signs of this amicable marriage. Inside, much of the cabinetry and woodwork received the same kind of artful attention that once led scholars to describe Craftsman style as "poetry in wood."

A Craftsman-style home was built on the premise that "wooden members should not be forced but shaped and fit together like pieces in a puzzle." The woven stairway is a classic example of this notion. Likewise, there is a common theme carried throughout the woodwork and interior finishes, from the light fixtures right on down to the fireplace screen.

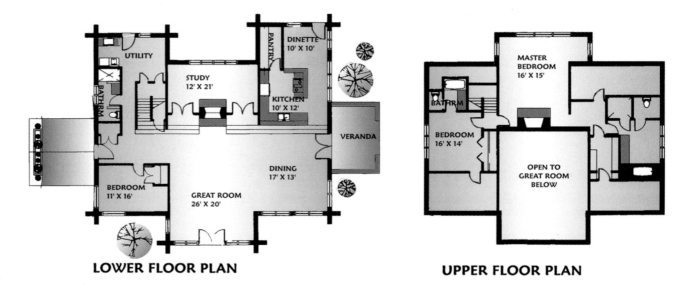

LOWER FLOOR PLAN　　　　　**UPPER FLOOR PLAN**

WRITE IT DOWN

Your house is not just about three bedrooms and two bathrooms. It's about who you are, how you live, and what you aspire to. Builder Jack McNamara advises would-be owners to write a "program." Take a good look in the mirror first, then get down to the particulars later. Beware of preconceived notions about what design should be.

The study, like the kitchen, is three stairs up from the main part of the home. One can enter through French doors on either side of the river-rock fireplace. This centrally located chimney services a second fireplace in the study and a third one upstairs in the master bedroom. Early on, there was talk of using full-round log walls to separate interior spaces. The concept was abandoned since both the architect and builder were after a lighter feel inside the house, along with a reasonable amount of flat wall space to accommodate artwork.

Timber-frame trusses frame the ceiling over the living room. For fun, the builders carved the home's birthday into one of the beams. Not wanting to overpower their beautiful wood with busy furnishings, the owners and interior decorator, Susan Niven, selected simple contemporary furnishings that complement the Craftsman theme running throughout the home.

WHAT'S SO HOT ABOUT COLD ROOFS?

In cold environments, ice dams that build up on roof eaves can damage shingles, tear off gutters and lead to leaks in the roof. They occur when warm air escapes from the roof and melts the snow on top. Water runs down to the uninsulated eaves and refreezes. The cycle repeats itself and the ice builds up. To prevent this destructive phenomenon, cold-climate homes frequently get topped with "cold roofs." These well-insulated roofs include venting systems that pull cool air in at the eaves and exhaust warm air through the ridge of the roof. While false ridges and Boston ridges are common, cupolas provide another stylish way to vent roofs.

—ART THIEDE,
WOODY'S LOG HOMES

At the heart of this home is an elevated kitchen that overlooks the dining area and great room. A friendly breakfast bar accommodates the cook's family and friends, while the counter in front serves to separate the kitchen from the living area below. It hides the clutter without hiding the cook. When viewed from the dining room, the counter functions as a display case for the family's dishes and collectibles.

CAMP DAVID

House plans for one piece of property were already underway when David discovered this lake-front oasis sited between two wetland areas. He knew this place was right just as surely as he'd known he would build with logs. Because of the sensitive nature of the lot, the building envelope was limited and access to the property was narrowly defined—facts he understood upon purchase. To help guard against the ruse of Mother Nature, a sump pump was placed in the basement along with an alarm system that will alert the security company should water creep in while David is away.

PHOTOS: GLEN CALVIN MOON, COURTESY OF MAPLE ISLAND LOG HOMES

CAMP DAVID
SIZE: 2,651 sq. ft.
MAIN FLOOR: 2,051 sq. ft.
UPPER FLOOR: 600 sq. ft.
LOG PRODUCER: Maple Island Log
    Homes
BUILDER: Scott Zoerhoff
ARCHITECT: Jack Begrow Architect, AIA

WHEN DAVID HAGELSTEIN set out to build a log house about ten years ago, friends tried to talk him out of it. They had heard the old stories and suggested that, at the very least, he build something framed then add log siding. David was sure that wouldn't be the same. He is a collector who relishes unique and finely crafted things. He knew innately what he wanted in his home and that only real logs would do!

Builder Scott Zoerhoff considers a house in progress to be more a work of art than a case of following instructions. Because of the size and variability of the logs, spaces tend to change when the walls go up. Sometimes, he says, you may have less space than you imagined, but often you have more. As such, he's a builder who doesn't mind change. He asks log producers not to fully pre-cut door and window openings, and just as soon as the walls and ceiling are up, he has a "parade." On site, the owner joins the electrician, plumber, heating, and air-conditioning specialists, the window people and so on. Boards are laid out on the floor to define interior spaces, and they all parade through the shell sharing thoughts and looking for potential problems or improvements. In David's house, all this fanfare led to some important changes, including the redesign and positioning of two masonry fireplaces.

BEFORE YOU BUY

Check the rules and regulations governing your land before you buy. Find out if your parcel is in the flood plain or at the base of an avalanche chute. Evaluate the building envelope and check on setbacks that dictate how far back you need to be from roads or water-ways. Don't forget to ask about planned outbuildings and fences too. Building codes and restrictions may have changed since the neighbor's house went up. Don't assume that you can do it just because the Joneses did.

A visit to David's log home leaves visitors guessing and marveling at his wonderful collection of the odd and unusual. David has long collected antiques and used them to invent spaces with a unique ambience and special warmth. Antique dressers replace conventional vanities in his bathroom, and a salvaged copper steam table in the kitchen is an intrigue at parties. Tiffany-type lamps and jeweled stained-glass fixtures from Plantation Galleries in Burton, Michigan, cast elegant light on the logs; David's rich red paisley couches are as welcoming as they are bold. An ancient pair of copper life preservers are perched on the logs in a whimsical interchange with the lakeside view.

UPPER FLOOR PLAN

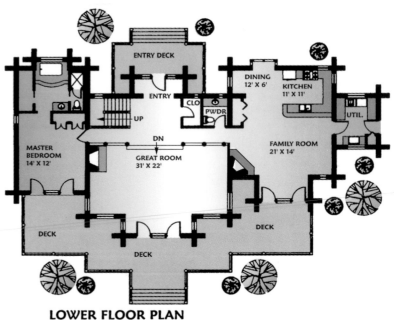

LOWER FLOOR PLAN

SECOND TIME AROUND

When Tom bought the ranch house, it contained around 900 square feet of living space. Over time, he grew a family and more than tripled the size of the house—all the while remaining sensitive to the home's historic character and original design. Log ends, protected by white corner boards, remained as they had been. Cracked mortar between the logs was replaced with flexible synthetic chink, but 'Forest Service brown' still colors the exterior. Maple red asphalt shingles are new but very much in keeping with the historic aesthetic.

PHOTOS: ROGER WADE, COURTESY OF LaCHANCE BUILDERS, INC.

SECOND TIME AROUND
SIZE: 2,980 sq. ft.
MAIN FLOOR: 1,640 sq. ft.
SECOND FLOOR: 1,340 sq. ft.
RESTORATION: LaChance Builders, Inc.
INTERIOR DESIGNER: Interiors by Catherine

Back in 1919, a self-sufficient ranching family laid claim to a remote chunk of land in Whitefish, Montana. There was no road to the property, so they grew a variety of crops, raised chickens and cows and pigs, operated a small sawmill, and even turned out their own tools and tractor parts on a steel lathe. When Tom LaChance purchased the property from the original owners in 1987, water was still retrieved by hand pump from a gravity-fed system. There was no insulation in the roof, and wood provided the main source of heat for warmth and cooking. Three bulbs supplied lighting for the entire house. Still, says Tom, "they'd done things right." The house sat on a sound foundation and the bones were good.

Over time, Tom modernized the house and added to it. He blended new into old so skillfully that you wouldn't know the difference. He added a little spit and polish to the outbuildings while recasting some with new purpose. The old smithy became a guest cottage; the bunkhouse was transformed into an exercise room. A larger building was added as company headquarters for LaChance Builders.

Tom increased the size of his living room by glassing in a screened porch on the back of the house. Upstairs, the addition of a large dormer transformed unlivable attic space into a comfortable master suite. There are no railings on the walk-out deck because Tom didn't need them obstructing his view. The pond was a bit of an experiment. With a river nearby, Tom knew that groundwater on the property was high, so he dug a small hole. As expected, it filled with water and stayed full. After observing the hole for nearly a year and a half, he dug a pond. Today, the pond is full of kids in the summer and trout year-round.

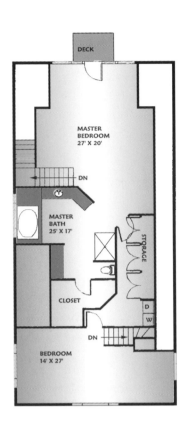

UPPER FLOOR PLAN

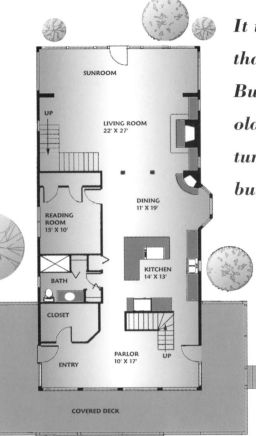

MAIN FLOOR PLAN

It usually costs more to restore a structure than it does to tear it down and start over. But there are charm and history about an old place that you won't completely recapture with new construction—even when you build with old materials.

WASH 'N' WEAR

Who says laundry rooms need to be downstairs? A washer and dryer near the bedrooms will save plenty of extra trips up and down those stairs. If you go this route, try to locate your machines where any noise is least likely to disturb your slumber.

Homesteaders often built with logs because they were readily available and free for the taking. Though practical, the perceived beauty of a log wall eluded many a pioneer wife. As a result, interior walls were often covered over with plaster and paint as soon as a family was able. This home was no exception, and half the fun was tearing all that stuff off the walls! Inside, a substantial new river-rock fireplace replaces the old yellow brick hearth. The chimney, however, was left in its original condition.

Hundred-year-old boards salvaged from falling-down sheds were re-planed and used in new kitchen cabinetry. Additional timbers were built into the ceiling to support the expanded living areas upstairs. Tom's floors were redone with wood from a hayloft owned by that famous American aviator Charles Lindbergh. Oh, if only they could talk!

When Tom puzzled over the finish details of his new staircase, he imagined a big pine bough blowing off a tree and landing right where the handrail should be. He conveyed this novel idea to local artisan Gregg Hanzel, who wrought this imaginary bough out of metal. The result is extraordinary, but a word of caution: local building codes vary substantially from community to community. In more restrictive areas, numerous details ranging from railing design and window size on down to the spacing of electrical receptacles are carefully dictated. In many areas, an open railing like this would not be permitted.

HAVENS, RETREATS & GRAND ESTATES

IT WASN'T SO LONG AGO when giants inhabited the dark woods—prehistoric, shaggy and coarse, yet gentle, magnificent and more awe-inspiring than any imaginary beast. These were the mighty cedars, firs, and redwoods of the Pacific Northwest. Averaging more than 300 feet in height with trunks spanning ten, sixteen, and twenty-two feet around, these were known simply as "the big trees." Famous remnants remain, but most are gone, and our impatient world has neither time nor space to grow them back. Though most of us can scarcely imagine such stature in a tree, that majesty of nature is imprinted here and there in American architecture. Perhaps we recall it best in the midst of our own national parks, where large logs (not really "the big trees," but big enough) are used in the design of grand lodges. Surely those works have helped inspire America's newfound penchant for bigger log homes. Neither always rustic nor predictable in their design, most of these contemporary log havens still link us to the earthly delights embodied by the tree.

"Whatever you can do, or dream you can, begin it. Boldness has genius, power and magic in it." **—GOETHE**

PHOTO: CINDY THIEDE AND JONATHAN STOKE

Built on a hill overlooking the lake, this unassuming elevation is as playful as it is charming. Designed by its artist owner in conjunction with the staff at Alpine Log Homes, it incorporates some unusual features. The second-floor dormer is decorated with a sunburst collar tie. A metal arch secured to a "tie" log spanning the gable end mirrors the circle-top window behind it. Posts that radiate out from the arch are attached to the purlins supporting the dormer roof. Notice, too, that the right side of the dormer roof sweeps down to meet the hip roof covering the broad porch—a practical feature that serves to divert snow and rain away from the entry.

PHOTOS: ROGER WADE, COURTESY OF ALPINE LOG HOMES

A peek from lakeside lends a whole new perspective to the cabin. The full walk-out basement supports the upper two stories on a striking foundation framed by three colorful stone archways. Ample green-trimmed windows and glass doors imbue this vacation retreat with antiquated cottage charm. Railed steps bushwhack down to the shore.

EVERYONE HAS HIS OR HER own vision of the quintessential log home. It may be a honey-colored retreat, dark brown lodge, or silver gray restoration. Whatever the look, it is achieved and maintained in part through the finish applied to the wood. This northern Wisconsin cabin recalls cottage estates and neighboring lakeside camps built near the turn of the twentieth century. Important features like divided light windows, painted trim, vintage dormers, and powerful stone accents imply historic character, but the weathered gray stain on the exterior suggests that, just maybe, this building's been here for awhile. (Ironically, contemporary log designs may use similar light colored stains to produce exactly the opposite effect.) There is another advantage too. Heavily pigmented finishes like this gray don't need to be applied as often as more transparent products that attempt to maintain the just-peeled look of new logs.

UP-NORTH WISCONSIN COTTAGE
SIZE: 3,700 sq. ft. (including full basement)
MAIN FLOOR: 1,500 sq. ft.
BASEMENT: 1,500 sq. ft.
UPPER FLOOR: 700 sq. ft.
DESIGNER AND LOG PRODUCER: Alpine Log Homes
CONTRACTOR: Rappa Construction

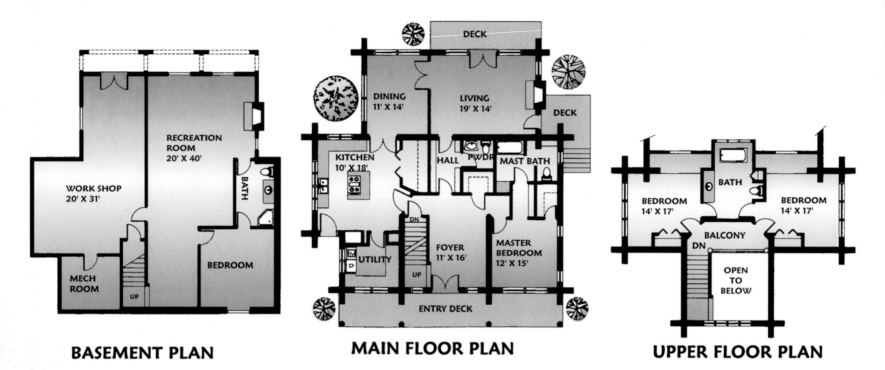

BASEMENT PLAN   **MAIN FLOOR PLAN**   **UPPER FLOOR PLAN**

"When selecting a finish for your home, don't scrimp on quality, and always follow the manufacturer's directions for proper application. Too often, people try to save time by spraying on a product that should be hand brushed. You may even want to apply an extra coat on more exposed southern and western elevations."

—TRESA KING, NORTHWEST CUSTOM LOG HOMES

A huge, old-fashioned foyer is the hub of this traditional design with each separate living space arranged in circular fashion around its core. You won't find a vaulted ceiling in this home's living room since the owners wanted intimacy there, but here in the entry, the welcome is grand.

Different northern Wisconsin seasons glow like picture postcards. In this year-round retreat, magical views of the lake and woods demanded large windows in every room. Even the kitchen forgoes upper cabinets in favor of wraparound views from ceiling to countertop. The light fixtures in the kitchen (and in most of the rest of the house) are rewired antiques. Salvaged marble atop the island is supported by an old gate post and two decorative wrought-iron brackets.

LOW-MAINTENANCE DESIGN

Logs are durable. Properly cared for, they will last far longer than you or I. The application of exterior finishes and preservatives is certainly one aspect of good maintenance, but proper design is the key to a truly low-maintenance home. Water and ultraviolet exposure are the bad guys. Start with a good foundation that keeps your lowest logs between twelve and eighteen inches off the ground. A twenty-four-inch roof overhang is okay. Thirty-six inches is even better since logs further down the wall will benefit too. Keep exposed log ends under cover, and fill any checks or cracks that threaten to catch or hold water. Log walls love porches, particularly on their most weather-beaten sides. Keep moisture-trapping shrubs and plantings a safe distance from your wood, and don't let misaimed sprinklers undermine your best-laid plan. A good gutter system will direct water away from your house and prevent roof drips from doing the old boomerang trick (splashing back from the ground onto the logs). Finally, keep in mind that log homes age differently, depending on the tree species, moisture content of the wood, and the microclimate around the home. While one house may need a new application of oil or preservative every three or four years, another might only need treatment every six, eight, or ten.

Arches are used repeatedly throughout this home. From the foyer, bold, round-top doors lead you through a unique book-lined passageway to the living room beyond.

An antique copper tub is tucked into the second-floor dormer. Knotty-pine walls are just what you'd expect in an "up north" vintage lake house. Elevated platforms like the one supporting this tub are commonly used in log homes where the second-story floor rests on ceiling logs visible from below. There is no hiding space for pipe, so the platform gives you room underneath to direct drain and water lines to your closest plumbing wall.

NORTHERN
EXPOSURE

In the early 1980s, the Swansons had a conventional home on Walloon Lake. It was filled to the brim with furniture handcrafted by Janet's dad, her own paintings and pictures, and the kinds of memories that imprint themselves in the very fabric of a home reserved for family gatherings. Sadly, in 1993, it was all destroyed by fire. While they couldn't replace what they had lost, they could create something different and, at least in terms of the building itself, something even better. The new house would be log, and unlike before, the bedrooms would be smaller and the gathering spaces much larger. The home fronts to the lake, where visitors are more likely to pull up in a boat than in a car. An eyebrow dormer is a distinctly historic feature that takes this home a notch back in time.

PHOTOS: ROGER WADE, COURTESY OF TOWN & COUNTRY CEDAR HOMES

NORTHERN EXPOSURE
SIZE: 3,450 sq. ft.
MAIN FLOOR: 1,725 sq. ft.
LOWER FLOOR: 1,725 sq. ft.
DESIGNER AND LOG PRODUCER: Town & Country
    Cedar Homes
BUILDER: Christopher J. Kuhn Custom Home Builder

"Logs represent seductive architectural details that compel you to go pick them."
—**STEPHEN BIGGS,** Town and Country Cedar Homes

For some families, a house in the city is necessary. It's where they work and, thus, where they must spend much of their time. It is not, however, always the most important home. When Steve and Janet Swanson's three grown children moved away, the couple relocated to "a funky little townhouse" in downtown Ann Arbor, Michigan. It's practical during the week, but it is not where their greatest investment lies nor where they spend their time when friends and family come. Instead, their emotional core is consummated with woven white cedar logs on the shores of Walloon Lake, three hours to the south. To call this a second home would somehow miss the mark.

Lakeside breezes fill this screened porch with the cool, sweet smells of summer. Should the weather dish up pelting rains instead, plastic curtains roll down for protection. In winter, the screens are replaced with Plexiglas and electric baseboard heat keeps this little niche warm and toasty. The rest of the house utilizes baseboard hot-water heat.

MYTH: LOG HOMES COST LESS TO BUILD THAN CONVENTIONAL STICK-FRAME HOMES

Steve Biggs, owner of Town and Country Cedar Homes, has been in the business of designing and building log homes for over twenty-five years. Steve will tell you that bargain hunters and practical shoppers who do their homework can succeed in building certain styles of log homes for prices comparable to, or sometimes less than, frame construction. But, he says (and it's a very big but), log homes are an art form, and art is not always practical! There are so many wonderful components to logs. When you're confronted with powerful entryways, full-scribe walls and corners, intricately notched stairways, or spacious cathedral ceilings, you'll want those things because it's what logs do. On the average, turn-key custom log homes tend to run between $125 and $150 per square foot. Manufactured kit homes can be considerably less, while hand-worked log packages finished to the nines can easily cost two to three times that amount.

Since the family's summer-home furnishings had perished in the fire, they had to start over completely. However, starting over didn't mean brand-"new." Rooms full of rustic antiques, bark-on furniture, and twig work smacks cozily of Adirondack camp style. From the light fixtures to the roll-away ladder that accesses extra-tall built-in bookshelves by the fieldstone fireplace, the cabin is awash in the colors and textures popularized by William West Durant when he developed those triumphant Adirondack Great Camp retreats late in the 1800s.

Rot-resistant and low-maintenance white cedar logs have some admirable qualities. They don't grow all that tall, however, and they tend to have a lot of taper. "You really have to work them," says Steve Biggs. He explains that Town and Country Cedar homes can still use white cedar to achieve the large log look, but when they stack them in the wall, they alternate the tips and butts. The resulting structure has a quirky woven quality with delightful personality. Since individual logs aren't lengthy enough to span particularly long sections of wall, posts are used intermittently.

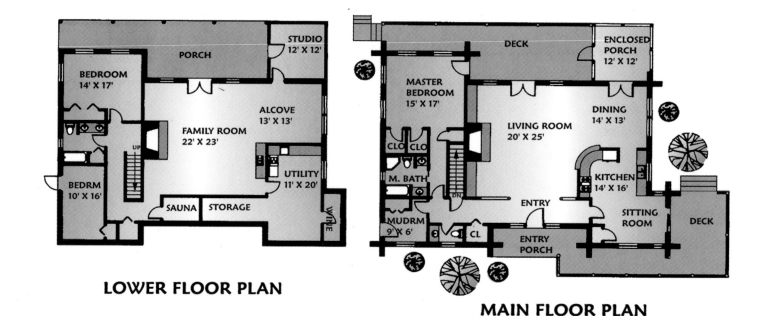

LOWER FLOOR PLAN

BEDROOM
14' X 17'

PORCH

STUDIO
12' X 12'

ALCOVE
13' X 13'

FAMILY ROOM
22' X 23'

UP

BEDRM
10' X 16'

UTILITY
11' X 20'

SAUNA   STORAGE

WINE

MAIN FLOOR PLAN

DECK

ENCLOSED
PORCH
12' X 12'

MASTER
BEDROOM
15' X 17'

LIVING ROOM
20' X 25'

DINING
14' X 13'

CLO CLO

M. BATH

DN

KITCHEN
14' X 16'

ENTRY

MUDRM
9' X 6'

CL

SITTING
ROOM

DECK

ENTRY
PORCH

Janet, an artist, has an eye for detail and fine craftsmanship. It is evident everywhere—particularly in the kitchen, with its twig work partition and murals of woodland scenes painted by the Swansons' daughter, Betsy. The design of the kitchen is one that improved as the house unfolded. The owners didn't want the space as closed in as the original plan suggested. Using sheets of Styrofoam, their builder, Chris Kuhn, helped them visualize what would have been and what could be. In the new arrangement, the wall between the kitchen and dining room was brought down to counter height. Twigging up above created separation without closing off the space. The refrigerator and kitchen cabinetry were moved into the area identified on the plan as the sitting room.

The old ranch buildings didn't have saddle-notched corners or dovetail notches. They had an easier geometry with squared-up logs and butt-and-pass corners. John and Nancy Carney claimed that general aesthetic for the new home, with one exception: their standing-dead logs were squared off on the inside and left round on the exterior. White-trimmed windows are reminiscent of the older dwellings, but John couldn't resist using one of his favorite tricks in the new house: windows were placed high on the walls to help direct sunlight deeper into the interior spaces.

PHOTOS: ROGER WADE

DOWN BY THE GREEN RIVER
SIZE: 4,100 sq. ft.
MAIN FLOOR: 2,960 sq. ft.
SECOND FLOOR: 1,140 sq. ft.
ARCHITECT: Carney Architects
BUILDER: On Site Management
LOG HOME PRODUCER: Pioneer Log Homes
INTERIOR DESIGNER: William Hodgins

THAT PLACE CALLED WYOMING is almost synonymous with the working ranch: horses, cows, and leather-faced cowboys with at least three days of stubble on their chins. Majestic, inspiring—yes, but not so important that you need to don a dinner jacket to eat out.

This is the place where a pre-eminent New York family sought solace from the city, and while they weren't necessarily look-ing for all the rough and tumble, they did want a house respectful of local ranching tradition. They pur-chased a large piece of range and

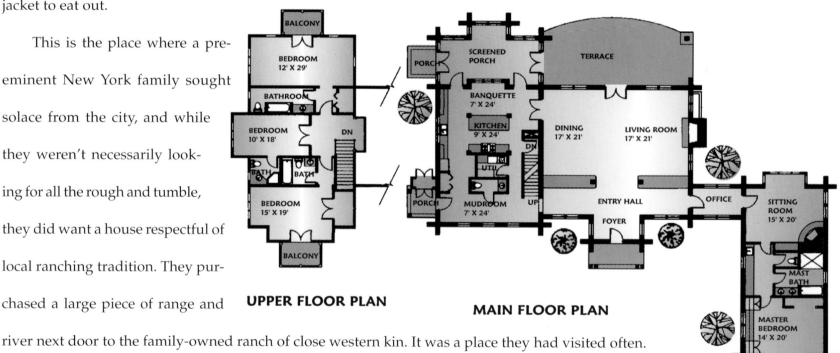

UPPER FLOOR PLAN

MAIN FLOOR PLAN

river next door to the family-owned ranch of close western kin. It was a place they had visited often.

The family invited their nephew John Carney and his wife, Nancy, to design their home. Since John's parents were the neighbors, he had an intimate working knowledge of the property. Wyoming's Green River flows through the heart of this land where a number of well-seasoned cabins and outbuildings are clustered near the riverbank. John and Nancy organized the site around those old buildings, fish-filled waters, and the nearby Wind River mountain range.

The house is large but not excessive. The owners wanted three guest bedrooms, a separate master suite, and a generous dining and living area, explains John, but they happily created crossover spaces in several areas when they could just as easily have tacked on an extra thousand feet. Soft, driftwoody colors texture the house with a few pop-out reds that are zesty and fun.

TOO BIG, TOO SMALL, JUST RIGHT

How much space is enough? While people can and do underbuild, designers and builders more often grapple with the tendency among wealthy clients to build larger homes than needed—or ultimately, than even wanted. Why make hard decisions about space when it's so easy to design in another room or a bigger closet? Well, most everyone is on a budget, so cost is one obvious reason not to overbuild. Care and maintenance of the home is another. However, less apparent may be the fact that big spaces tend to be less livable. People build for the eventuality of a million visiting relatives while forgetting that all those aunts, uncles, cousins, kids, and grandkids may only be there a few weeks out of the year. Then what?

The roof and second story are framed with timber trusses stained the same muted color as the log walls. Whitewashed ceilings add to the bright open feel of the space. A full masonry chimney outside the home looks dry-stacked and is appropriately built with "farmer's rock." Inside, however, the owners wanted the fireplace downplayed (no buffalo heads above this mantel!). They chose a buff-colored sandstone that matched the radiant-heat floors, then used an interesting architectural piece up top.

Relationships between family and staff tend to be more formal in the East. Here, the mood is much more casual and relaxed. This cheery yellow kitchen is well equipped and roomy enough for the cook to putter behind the high-backed island while friends or family share a snack around the farmhouse table with its built-in bench. The floor is laid with old-fashioned Dutch-made linoleum. It's practically bomb proof!

This timber-frame screened porch overlooks some of the classic old barn and shed structures built back when the ranch was all business. The Green River is also very close, and it's not unusual to see a cow moose and calf foraging through the riverside thickets.

"In most areas, a well-built log home will appreciate faster than a comparable frame home—regardless of what the land is doing underneath it."

—GREG STECKLER, LOG RHYTHMS

Log home designers and builders glean much from traditional architecture. That, however, has merely been their starting point. Designers continually push the envelope with intricate designs that, among other things, incorporate huge expanses of glass. Builders have risen to meet the challenge, but not without some impressive advancements in technology and engineering. Log walls tend to be less stabile the higher up they go. The sheer weight of a tall wall will also cause significant settling, even if the house is built with dry logs. To that, add the fact that walls are severely weakened when so much of the wood is cut away to make room for soaring window walls. To stabilize the walls and restore structural integrity, builders incorporate sophisticated systems of steel rods, connectors, and plates embedded inside the walls and posts of a structure.

PHOTO: TIM HERBERT

ELKHEAD LODGE
SIZE: 6,200 sq. ft.
MAIN FLOOR: 3,200 sq. ft.
UPPER FLOOR: 1,000 sq. ft.
LOWER FLOOR: 2,000 sq. ft.
DESIGNER AND LOG PRODUCER:
  Alpine Log Homes
BUILDER: Beck & Associates

This second-floor balcony fringes the great room below. It is, in effect, suspended from the impressive, double-cord log trusses supporting the roof. Brawny metal brackets are structural and their presence suggests strength and power. Upstairs, three bedrooms and a bunk room open off the balcony like guest rooms in an old western lodge.

PHOTOS UNLESS NOTED: DANN COFFEY, COURTESY OF ALPINE LOG HOMES

NATIONAL PARKS IN AMERICA are synonymous with majesty and splendor. You don't walk away from a visit without taking along grand memories of the wildlife, mountain vistas, and spectacular old lodges—many of which were built from logs. It was, in fact, these very lodges that conspired with America's subconscious, convincing her to give log home living a second chance. As such, these national masterpieces are frequently remembered in contemporary log home architecture. That was true of this robust retreat handcrafted by Alpine Log Homes. It took more than four months to pre-build the shell and roof structure in Alpine's log yard, but only a week to re-erect it on a readied foundation near Vail, Colorado.

The owners call this grand estate Elkhead Lodge after the impressive creature that, for them, has come to symbolize the mountain lifestyle. Inside, elk are remembered nearly everywhere you look, from the mount above the mantel to the fireplace screen, antler floor lamp, and custom-designed light fixtures throughout the house.

BUGGED BY IT ALL

Log homes have that sometimes-deserved reputation of being particularly attractive to insects such as flies and wasps. Since logs retain heat, insects seek them out, and it doesn't take so much as a peephole to let them in. The problem, however, lies less with the logs than with the overall construction of the building. A stable, well-sealed home will not cater to hordes of dead and dying flies on the windowsills. But a gap in any home is a potential doorway for bugs, and because logs will shift and settle over time, new gaps may develop. While companies always allow for settling, a crack is still a crack. Tongue-and-groove decking that butts up against walls in the gable ends is one spot to watch and seal. Corner notching and the fit around doors and windows are others. If gaps develop later (and it's always good to let your home settle for a few seasons), they can be resealed with caulk or chink. In other cases, builders apply insecticide mixed in with the final finish coat on exterior log walls. There are other options, too, including topical sprays and treatments applied to the soil around the home where insects breed. For more information, contact companies like Perma-chink and Weatherall who specialize in log-home preservatives, sealants, stains and finishes.

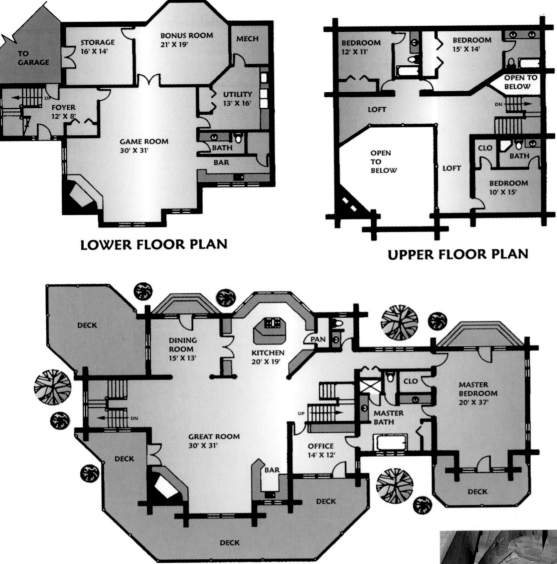

LOWER FLOOR PLAN

- TO GARAGE
- STORAGE 16' X 14'
- BONUS ROOM 21' X 19'
- MECH
- FOYER 12' X 8'
- UTILITY 13' X 16'
- GAME ROOM 30' X 31'
- BATH
- BAR

UPPER FLOOR PLAN

- BEDROOM 12' X 11'
- BEDROOM 15' X 14'
- OPEN TO BELOW
- LOFT
- DN
- OPEN TO BELOW
- CLO
- BATH
- LOFT
- BEDROOM 10' X 15'

MAIN FLOOR PLAN

- DECK
- DINING ROOM 15' X 13'
- KITCHEN 20' X 19'
- PAN
- DECK
- GREAT ROOM 30' X 31'
- DN
- UP
- MASTER BATH
- CLO
- MASTER BEDROOM 20' X 37'
- DECK
- BAR
- OFFICE 14' X 12'
- DECK
- DECK
- DECK

Whatever happened to laundry chutes? Grandma had one. Given various trade-offs in room layout, you can't always squeeze them in at just the right spot, but when the bedrooms are upstairs and the laundry is in the basement, think gravity, and reap the rewards of persistent planning!

The master bedroom occupies a wing of its own. It is purposefully located away from the primary living areas and guest bedrooms. A second stone fireplace has a sandstone hearth and mantel—the same material used on all the window ledges. Lighting in the lodge is supplied by the increasingly popular and safe low-voltage system that lets you operate your lights, heat, and appliances with the touch of a button—from your home, the office, or the plane you fly in on.

KWAHU

This super-insulated home takes a number of traditional and revolutionary approaches to energy efficiency. The upper level employs in-floor radiant heat, but that is just the beginning. A solar space comprising two stories and more than 600 square feet captures warm air from above and circulates it down through a concrete air core under the house. This system serves to heat the lower level of the home while maintaining comfortable temperatures in each sun space. In addition, two sealed combustion-air fireplaces draw outside air into the firebox, heat it, then circulate it throughout the living spaces. The double-thick, insulated, standing-seam steel roof has an R-value approaching 72, while the walls are rated at R-38! (R-values for a typical frame home in a comparable climate might be 40 and 20 respectively.)

PHOTOS: BOB FRANZESE

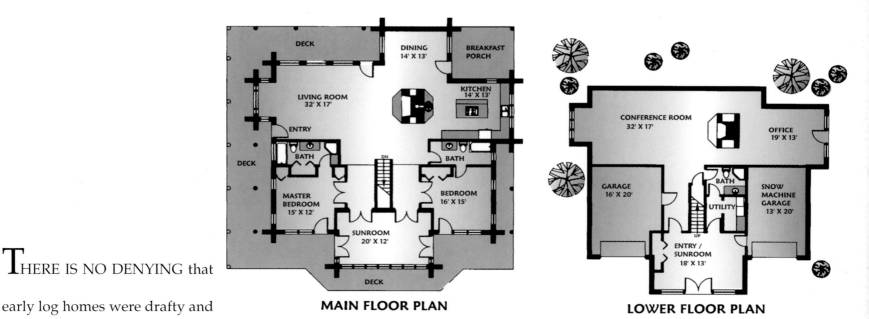

MAIN FLOOR PLAN   **LOWER FLOOR PLAN**

THERE IS NO DENYING that early log homes were drafty and cold. Most pioneer builders didn't understand all the ramifications of settling, nor did they have modern-day synthetic, elastic chinking compounds. Today, contemporary builders stake their reputations on weather-tight homes. The result, according to recent surveys by the Log Home Living Association in Chantilly, Virginia, is a worldwide industry that pumps out more than a billion dollars worth of homes each year. However, more difficult than reinventing the technology was the process of convincing the buying public that logs homes were, indeed, energy efficient. As a result, some companies have gone over the top to produce building systems that will out-compete and out-perform nearly any available structure on the market with a door and two windows.

Super-insulated "sandwich wall" construction is one of those systems. Developed by Logcrafters of Pinedale, Wyoming, the construction of a home starts with D-shaped logs. Next comes the filling—vapor barriers, insulation and a stud wall. The sandwich is finished off with a thinner layer of round log siding. The walls look like solid log, but the framed section in between is a sure-fire guarantee that warm air stays in—or out, depending on the season.

KWAHU
SIZE: 4,150 sq. ft.
MAIN FLOOR: 2,500 sq. ft.
LOWER FLOOR: 1,650 sq. ft. plus two garages with 600 sq. ft. of space
DESIGNER AND BUILDER: Logcrafters, Pinedale, Wyoming

MYTH: LOG HOMES ARE LESS ENERGY-EFFICIENT THAN STICK-BUILT HOMES

The energy efficiency of a home has traditionally been expressed in terms of "R-value." The rating measures a material's resistance to the transfer of heat from one side to another. According to conventional standards, the higher the R-value, the better. Because logs absorb and store heat, they have a relatively low R-value. In the past, that fact forced producers to overbuild just to meet code. Today, however, it is widely acknowledged that the true efficiency potential of a log has more to do with its thermal mass, or its ability to absorb, store, and release heat over time. Logs do this well. In fact, conclusive studies now show that although the R-value for log walls may be 44 percent lower than for frame walls, log houses are every bit as energy efficient! It's also worth noting that while a four-inch-thick log will not be as efficient as an eight-inch log, it will perform to code even in the coldest climates. The real key to performance lies less with the size of the log than with the construction of an airtight wall. So, pick a log because you like the way it looks, then build tight.

The owners probably spend nine months a year in this secluded Wyoming home, where winter access demands a seven-mile trek in on snowmobiles. The kitchen and other main living areas in the house are located on the upper level, while the garage, front entry, and a considerable amount of office space is tucked down below. The Southwest Door Company built the doors and windows from hand-brushed cedar and all the cabinet faces from cedar and saguaro cactus panels. Doors just left of the oven look like pantry doors, but you will find the refrigerator behind them.

Technology and energy efficiency combine to make this Wyoming retreat a tribute to contemporary log home design. In addition to its sandwich-wall construction, the house incorporates the increasingly popular computer-regulated, low-voltage control system that gives the owners mastery over their lights, heat, security system, appliances, and more from most anywhere in the world. This smart-house system also provides infinitely more efficient and programmable in-home lighting options. Turn all the lights in the house off with the touch of a button, or program preset scenes for function or mood.

DESIGNED WITH A VIEW

The prow front of this alpine home incorporates massive roof overhangs that help shade the interiors from abundant summer sun without blocking the view. The overhangs and covered porches further protect the logs from the weather and the degrading effect of ultraviolet radiation on the wood.

PHOTOS: COURTESY OF NORTHWEST CUSTOM HOMES

DESIGNED WITH A VIEW
SIZE: 3,460 sq. ft.
MAIN FLOOR: 2,200 sq. ft.
SECOND FLOOR: 1,260 sq. ft.
LOG PRODUCER AND BUILDER:
    Northwest Custom Log Homes, Inc.
DESIGNER: Log Rhythms, Inc.

Flagstone pavers and an artisan-crafted glass-and-copper door promote elegance in the front entry. Dead-standing lodgepole pine was used to construct this home using the full-scribe Scandinavian technique. In this style of construction, the logs fit tightly together so there is no chinking.

THOUGH A GRAND VIEW quite often determines the basic layout of a home, its mass and flavor will evolve over time. This home underwent no fewer than twenty-eight revisions during a design process that was perceived by its owners, designer, and builder not as tedious, but exhilarating! In the end, the large prow front was rounded out to make better use of the interior space. Cathedral ceilings and a huge loft that doubles as a family room are organized around a vista that encompasses the entire Cascade mountain range.

Like any home, a log house gathers dust. It's a problem that gets bigger with the height of your cathedral ceiling. Rough-peeled logs will make your job more troublesome than smooth, well-sanded walls, since they tend to eat cleaning rags then display the shredded bits for all the world to see. On the other hand, roughed up logs probably won't show the dirt!

FINANCING YOUR DREAM

Times are changing and log homes have more credibility now than ever before. Still, there are lending institutions that remain uncomfortable with log construction for one reason or another. Before you start, prequalify yourself. How much do you earn each year and how much debt do you carry? Those numbers will determine how much money you're qualified to borrow. Be realistic about your budget and what a reasonable allotment will be for your land. If you have $250,000 to spend, you probably can't afford a $100,000 lot. Ask log home producers for their recommendations. Most reputable companies have been involved with homes financed by various lenders. Not only can they direct you to supportive lending institutions, but those entities can lend with more confidence when they know your builder is stable and quality conscious.

An extra-deep balcony runs the length of the house behind the vaulted prow. Though open, the space manages to incorporate niches and nooks for different purposes. One cozy sitting area centers around a woodstove flued into the main fireplace.

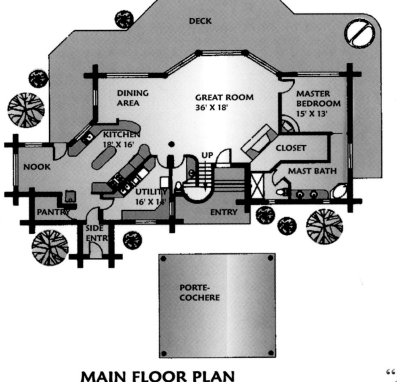

MAIN FLOOR PLAN

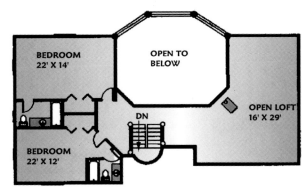

UPPER FLOOR PLAN

"Plan the work and work the plan." —ANONYMOUS

DESIGN GOES HIGH-TECH

An echo heard round the industry goes something like this: Time and/or money invested in the planning process is well spent, indeed! It will, in fact, save you money later. Because designers and builders know this, they are always striving to make the design process easier and more visual for their clients. Computer-aided design is becoming an increasingly popular tool that allows you to modify designs with ease. Walls can even be drawn in 3-D. Some companies are taking this all a step further. Log Rhythms, Inc., one of a number of up-and-coming computer-design firms, is producing 3-D computer-aided models from log home plans. The models are translated into video that you can watch at home. These computer-generated movies allow you to walk around the house or through it! They may help you avoid costly mistakes or cinch design decisions that would, otherwise, be hard to picture. The process is time consuming and currently costs about fifty cents per square foot of house. But given the scale and complexity of some of today's custom log homes, it is not too much to pay.

A covered carport, or porte cochere, is a practical design feature for homes with detached garages or none at all. You can park at least four cars under this one! Extra-thick, architectural-grade asphalt shingles on the roof come with a forty-year guarantee.

ALPINE
MEADOWS

Extensive research had convinced one owner that a manufactured log house was the way to go. His wife, however, wanted something more traditional and handcrafted. This Bridger Mountain design seemed like the perfect compromise. Ten-inch milled logs were given the once-over with a drawknife to add homespun appeal. The logs are Swedish-coped and stacked with saddle-notched corners. To guard against wayward air leaks as the house settles, two strips of polyurethane foam are laid in the cope lines between the logs. While this method of building eliminates the need for chinking, the owners opted for it because it gives further insurance against air infiltration, and they like the way it looks.

PHOTOS: ROGER WADE, COURTESY OF BRIDGER MOUNTAIN LOG HOMES UNLESS NOTED OTHERWISE

ALPINE MEADOWS
SIZE: 4,450 sq. ft. plus garage
MAIN FLOOR: 1,800 sq. ft.
SECOND FLOOR: 1,350 sq. ft.
LOWER FLOOR: 1,300 sq. ft. plus a 400-sq.-ft. garage
DESIGNER AND LOG PRODUCER: Bridger Mountain
    Log Homes
BUILDER: Stan Yung Construction

PEOPLE ARE DRAWN TO LOGS by the warmth and aesthetic of the wood. In fact, people used to be so enamored with the idea of log walls that they tended to use them everywhere—not just on the outside, but for all their interior partition walls as well. The result could be overpowering and leave the house feeling dark and closed in.

Another common mistake was to overlook the depth of the wood when laying out the floor plans. Since big logs take up far more space than framed walls, homeowners occasionally found themselves with pinched-in rooms and closets. Today, experienced log home designers don't make those mistakes, but they still may opt for interior log walls. The difference is that contemporary floor plans accommodate large logs with bigger rooms, free-flowing spaces, light colored finishes, and plenty of windows. In this home designed by Bridger Mountain Log Homes and built by their affiliate, Stan Yung Construction, the owners wanted plenty of wood. They didn't have a lot of fine art needing to be displayed on clean white walls. Instead, they opted for a spacious home that emphasized the beauty of the logs.

Having been forced to move fifteen times during their working years, the owners embraced the thought of spending their retirement in a home that was both permanent and tailored specially for them. The home sits atop a walk-out daylight basement that includes not only a guest room, large family area, and laundry room, but a third garage in addition to the other two attached at the home's main level by a covered breezeway. Radiant heat is used on all three levels and covered with wood floors specifically approved for in-floor heating systems. A four-season gazebo off to the side of the house has removable glass panels that are replaced with screens in summer, and its small kitchenette makes entertaining a pleasure.

PHOTO: BRIDGER MOUNTAIN LOG HOMES

"Here in Montana," says the owner, "there are eight
months of winter and four months of compan[...]
family kitchen stands in testimony to th[...]
talents and delights of the cook. When the f[...]
planning the home, they took their list of [...]
pleasures to a company that specialized in [...]
design. The result was this beautiful and gra[...]
space that lacks for nothing. The island is fourtee[...] feet
long and culminates in a large octagonal dining bar.
A second fridge and icemaker, microwave, and additional garbage space are located underneath. A wine
cooler is built into the counter on the left, and there
are an abundance of storage spaces and pullout drawers concealed behind finely crafted cabinetry.

TIME . . . TIME . . . TIME

*Rome wasn't built in a day, and it certainly wasn't
furnished in a week. Allow yourself plenty of time
to shop around and compare various products.
Character is built over time, so have patience
when it comes to choosing your building materials
as well as your furnishings. Above all, consider
costs, but don't overlook quality.*

The baby grand piano in the loft is visible from the great room below. The instrument is the
wife's pride and her family's joy when she fills the house with music. Moving the piano into
place, however, was a major chore. The stairway was wide enough at the base, but log ends
protruding into the stairwell several feet up blocked passage when movers lifted the piano
into the air. In the end, they had to construct a ramp and pull it up. The acoustics are
excellent, due in part to the open design of the house, a fourteen-inch- thick, well-insulated
roof, and the logs themselves.

RADIANT WARMTH

Radiant heat, or, more accurately, in-floor heating, is a pleasant, clean, and increasingly popular way to heat log homes. Why? For one thing, you don't have to worry about concealing extensive ductwork amidst log walls (unless, of course, your climate also demands air-conditioning). For another, the thermal properties of logs cause warm air to move very slowly through the walls. Once logs warm up, they stay that way and do a super job of keeping the air temperature constant. Initially, the system will cost more to install, but if you plan on living in your home for a long time, lower operating costs will even out the bill within a few years. Your home will also take longer to warm up when you first turn up the thermostat, but you have the added advantage of separating living spaces into zones that can be regulated independent of one another. You can't do that with forced-air systems unless you add a second furnace.

Stone and tile flooring work best with radiant heat. Wood is popular too, but you may need to operate your system at a lower temperature to keep the wood from over-drying and shrinking or splitting. Even that is likely, however, since the quality and efficiency of the heat make it possible to set your thermostat four to seven degrees cooler without sacrificing comfort.

Stan's crew stained and sealed the outside of this home as soon as the logs were up and the roof was on. Inside, however, the sun started to discolor the wood before the interior finish could be applied. Because the owners had selected a light stain, the builder was afraid that the uneven coloration would show through. Instead of sacrificing quality, the contractor opted to re-sand all the interior walls. His bid, however, never changed, not then nor in the sixteen months it took to build this home.

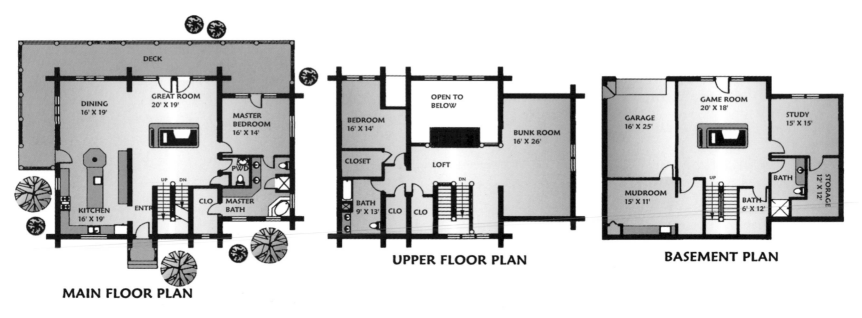

MAIN FLOOR PLAN

DECK

DINING 16' X 19'

GREAT ROOM 20' X 19'

MASTER BEDROOM 16' X 14'

PWD

UP DN

KITCHEN 16' X 19'

ENTRY

CLO

MASTER BATH

UPPER FLOOR PLAN

OPEN TO BELOW

BEDROOM 16' X 14'

BUNK ROOM 16' X 26'

CLOSET

LOFT

BATH 9' X 13'

CLO CLO

DN

BASEMENT PLAN

GARAGE 16' X 25'

GAME ROOM 20' X 18'

STUDY 15' X 15'

MUDROOM 15' X 11'

UP

BATH 6' X 12'

BATH

STORAGE 12' X 12'

MOUNTAIN TRACING

Pay close attention to any special rules governing the land on which you plan to build. Subdivisions can dictate larger or smaller homes, depending on where you live. When architect David Gibson discovered that the decks of this split-level home were larger than local building codes allowed, he notched out the corners, then filled the void with rock planters flanking the garage. The result, says the owner, was a better design overall! The planters give substance to the front of the house while making the garage doors seem less prominent.

PHOTOS: DAVID MARLOW

The liberal use of beveled glass is one of this home's hallmarks. In the entry, geometric patterns of glass are accentuated by dark trim. As the sun sets, the glass sends prisms of patterned light dancing across the log walls and floor inside the foyer.

MOUNTAIN TRACING
SIZE: 3,200 sq. ft.
MAIN FLOOR: 2,400 sq. ft.
LOWER FLOOR: 800 sq. ft. plus 750-sq.-ft.
  garage
LOG PRODUCER: Custom Log Homes
BUILDER: Norris & Associates
ARCHITECT: David Gibson, Gibson Reno
  Architects

ARE LOG HOMES MORE EXPENSIVE than conventional stick-built homes? Perhaps they are, but architect David Gibson believes you get so much more for your money! He talks about mass and longevity and the natural beauty inherent in the wood. Those qualities, it seems, also endear log homes to the land. What, then, would be more fitting than to pattern a home's design after the inspiring mountain peaks it overlooks? This prominent, multi-gabled roofline does just that. The gables not only emulate the distant Colorado peaks, but the point of each gable aims directly at the tallest peak, framing it in each window wall. You connect instantly!

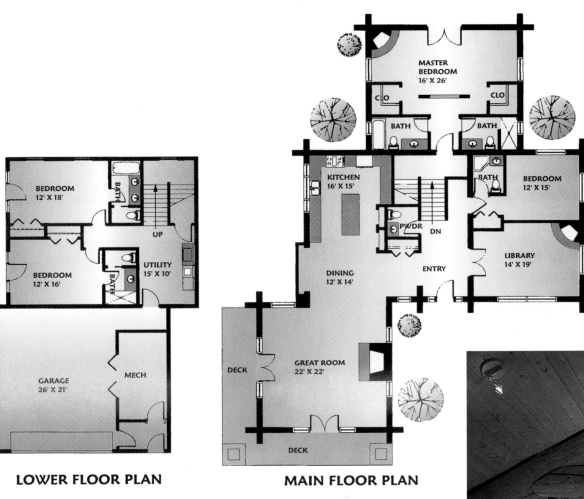

LOWER FLOOR PLAN

BEDROOM
12' X 18'

BATH

UP

BEDROOM
12' X 16'

BATH

UTILITY
15' X 10'

GARAGE
26' X 21'

MECH

MAIN FLOOR PLAN

MASTER
BEDROOM
16' X 26'

CLO

CLO

BATH

BATH

KITCHEN
16' X 15'

BATH

BEDROOM
12' X 15'

PWDR

DN

DINING
12' X 14'

ENTRY

LIBRARY
14' X 19'

DECK

GREAT ROOM
22' X 22'

DECK

Logs glow rich and warm as the setting sun turns the night sky a deep and magic blue. Mount Daley peaks at 12,000 feet on the horizon. Upper courses of log ends protruding into the opening between the dining area and this great room are sculpted to create a dramatic corbeled entryway.

The same sun you covet in winter can be uncomfortably warm in summer. Cool down your interiors by planting deciduous trees near those seasonal hot spots. According to the U.S. Department of Energy, trees planted outside south-facing windows can reduce the temperature by as much as 9 degrees in the surrounding areas. Then in winter, when the leaves have dropped, the sun can shine through again in all its warming glory.

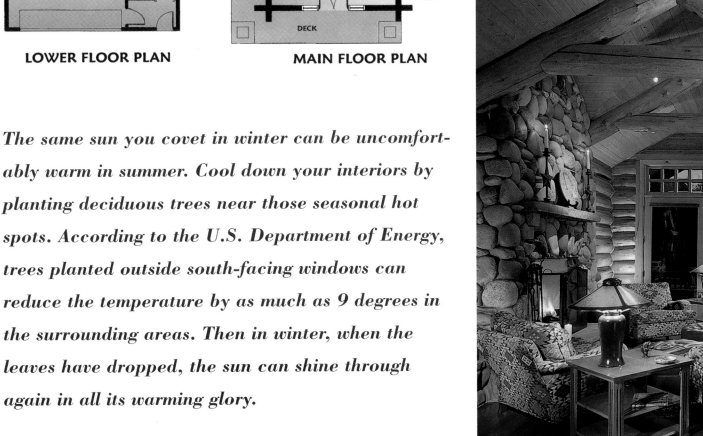

WHAT'S COOKING IN YOUR KITCHEN?

Breakfast—family conversation and daily plans. Lunch—book work, taxes, and a new dress for the prom. Dinner—homework, vacation planning, and entertaining with the neighbors. Today's kitchens are so much more than sinks, stoves, and refrigerators. While good design may start with the classic work triangle, it will also account for traffic flows, adequate storage and counter space, and, perhaps, the possibility of more than one cook. Typically, a well-planned kitchen arrangement puts the refrigerator, cooktop, and sink in a triangle where the total distance between appliances is no more than seven feet. Variety, however, is the key, and while this classic approach may still apply, multi-cook families might add workstations outside the triangle, or modify it with the addition of central islands and wider aisles. How 'bout your kitchen?

• Do you share the cooking and cleanup? • Do you like the morning sun? • Do you have at least twelve feet of counter space? • Can you open your dishwasher and still get to your sink? • Is there space for dishes and flatware near the dishwasher? • Will an open fridge block traffic or get in the way of the sink or cooktop? • Do you want an informal dining area or breakfast bar? • Have you thought about a walk-in pantry, overhead pot rack, recycling center, desk, or appliance garage? • Do you have adequate task lighting arranged in zones that can be turned on and off separately? • Is there a clear three-foot path throughout the kitchen? • Can the cook see the guests? Can the guests see the dirty dishes? Do you care?

Appliances are out of sight in this kitchen, where richly crafted cherry-wood cabinets disguise an oversized refrigerator against the back wall. An under-counter oven is built into the far end of the kitchen island, while the front of that island displays an ornate fire plate originally intended to absorb and radiate heat from a fireplace. The elaborate metal pot rack overhead started out as a widow's walk—most likely from the rooftop of a seaside home.

While log home design often compels great cavernous spaces, smaller "close-off" rooms might rise to the top of a homeowner's list of favorite places to spend their time. Antique leaded-glass doors buffer this comfortable den from the cacophony of household chatter. The doors, however, came first—a treasured find that inspired the design of this special niche.

SKY RANCH

The Timmerhus crew built their "new old house" from green wood. True to the home's make-believe history, they employed Swedish full-scribe construction, where one green log is carefully scribed to the next. As the wood dries, the logs shrink together for a tighter fit. The owners chose eastern white pine for building because the wood tends to be more stable over time. Since this house was born in Colorado then transplanted to the arid Southwest, they knew it would shrink substantially. The owners didn't want clean logs, so the crew "skip-peeled" them. All the doors and windows were custom designed then built on site from recycled wood.

PHOTOS: PETER BLOOM (HORIZONS WEST)

"RANCH VERNACULAR—something that had always been there": that's how the owners described their house vision to the group of freewheeling artisans who would design and build it. To move the concept along, the group invented a story. Once upon a time, there was this Swedish fellow—an immigrant rancher who dropped anchor in Arizona. He built his original log ranch house from scratch using old-world craftsmanship. He crafted a hammer-beam truss in his living room—something akin to a medieval English church truss. But being a cowboy and all, he gave it a western twist and combined hewn timbers with round, skip-peeled logs. Later he threw up some porches and built on a stick-frame addition. The ranch prospered, so he kept on building. He added stone; he built with different log styles. He put a big ol' roof on to tie it all together. Eventually he built a timber-frame barn and a stone garage, then connected them together with covered walks. The old place got newer but never lost its sense of history!

SKY Ranch
SIZE: 3,400 sq. ft.
MAIN FLOOR: 2,500 sq. ft.
UPPER FLOOR: 900 sq. ft.
LOG PRODUCER AND BUILDER:
    Timmerhus
ARCHITECT: Paul Froncek, AIA

One gander at this stone fireplace will convince you that it isn't something you see every day. Built-in sitting areas (borrowed from some of Mary Colter's Grand Canyon architecture) are just part of the intrigue. Look up and you'll notice a pass-through arch. Stairs to the second floor are located behind the fireplace. You walk up from behind and circle around to the front, where you can lean over the railing and wave to anybody seated below—or continue on around through the arch and onto a bridge leading to the second-floor bedrooms. Because the arch is located directly above the fireplace, the flue splits in two with sections of pipe running up both sides of the arch.

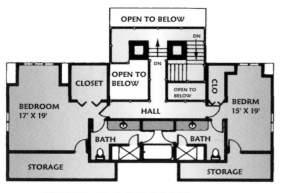

UPPER FLOOR PLAN

BEDROOM 17' X 19'

CLOSET

OPEN TO BELOW

DN

OPEN TO BELOW

OPEN TO BELOW

CLO

BEDRM 15' X 19'

HALL

DN

BATH

BATH

STORAGE

STORAGE

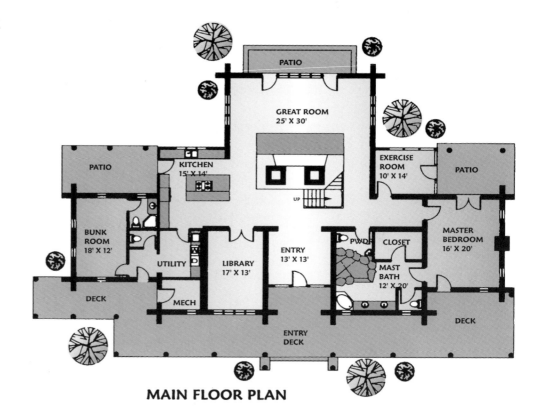

MAIN FLOOR PLAN

PATIO

GREAT ROOM 25' X 30'

PATIO

KITCHEN 15' X 14'

EXERCISE ROOM 10' X 14'

PATIO

UP

BUNK ROOM 18' X 12'

UTILITY

LIBRARY 17' X 13'

ENTRY 13' X 13'

PWDR

CLOSET

MASTER BEDROOM 16' X 20'

MAST BATH 12' X 20'

DECK

MECH

ENTRY DECK

DECK

MYTH: LOG HOMES ARE MORE SUSCEPTIBLE TO FIRE THAN OTHER TYPES OF CONSTRUCTION

If log homes seem more susceptible to fire, it's probably because they tend to be located in remote locations where early detection may be hindered or firefighters are just too darn far away. The truth is, a log wall with any mass to it will not ignite as readily as one that is framed.

What is it about a great big walk-in shower? The owners had always wanted one and the crew had always wanted to build one. They chose "malapai"— an indigenous flat rock, hand-picked by permit off national forest land. Only one problem: if the rock gets wet, it will eventually grow moss. They solved the problem by using hand-painted tiles back in the spray zone. The sink basins are also hand-painted—one with the portraits of the family's three young huskies—Spirit, Kowboy, and Yukon: hence, the name SKY Ranch.

"You've got to enjoy the journey!" —OWNERS **LISA SHOVER AND JERRY KACKLEY**

WILL MY LOGS SHRINK OR SETTLE?

They might do both, but there is a difference. Fresh-cut, or "green," wood has a high moisture content. As the wood dries out, it shrinks. A log house built with green logs will shrink substantially, so the home is designed and engineered with that in mind. On the other hand, homes built with dead-standing trees may not shrink, but they will shift and settle. Settling is more likely to be affected by weighty loads. The higher the walls, the heavier the roof, and the more settling you can expect.

The kitchen is one of those framed-in sections that lends credence to the tale that this prosperous ranching family needed more room somewhere along the way. Finished with rough-sawn boards and outfitted with hand-distressed and painted cabinets, this room could be an updated holdover from an 1800s farmhouse. Greg Peters of Rysso-Peters did the painting—all eleven layers!

KAMP KRUEGER

Mickey and Lori had never built a house before, much less a log one. The clincher was a television show that featured Maple Island Log Homes building an actual cabin. The place was small but charming. "We wanted that house," says Lori. Of course, once they started the design process, their floor plan grew some, then grew some more. It's large, but for this family who spends their week in an 1,800-square-foot apartment, it's just right. Big spaces deliberately open up to little spaces, and there are two sunrooms on opposite sides of the home. Because the Kruegers' children are young, they rejected the suggestion to put the master bedroom on the main floor away from other sleeping areas. "When we get old, we'll just have to walk upstairs," says Lori. In the meantime, the kids come first.

PHOTOS: PAUL ROCHELEAU, COURTESY OF MAPLE ISLAND LOG HOMES

Did you know that the seed of the giant redwood is only 1/16 of an inch across?
You would need 123,000 of them to fill a one-pound bag.

KAMP KRUEGER
SIZE: 3,400 sq. ft. plus an attached 725-sq.-ft. garage
MAIN FLOOR: 2,240 sq. ft
UPPER FLOOR: 1,160 sq. ft.
LOG PRODUCER: Maple Island Log Homes
DESIGNER: Gordon Hughes, Maple Island Log
     Homes and Joan Humphries, A + H Architects

THE BIG APPLE IS THE CITY to beat all cities. Fast-paced, cultured, diverse, productive: it is all of those things and more. Still, the city is the city. Young children in a Manhattan apartment don't just jump on their bikes and ride around the neighborhood. For Mickey and Lori Krueger's family, a log home on ten wooded acres outside New York is what was missing. Their spacious, "every weekend" retreat provides more than just an escape—it lends balance to their family life. It's the place where their kids can run through the woods, roll in the grass, and scale the side of the fireplace!

"Big rooms call for large, overstuffed couches and chairs to make them cozy," says Lori. But the family is also amused by friends who, not having been in a log home before, thought the house felt "done" long before it was. "It's the wood in the walls. Sometimes they just stand there with their mouths open!" The fireplace also gets your attention. It is so massive, says Mickey, that the great room could actually have been bigger. Log homes are different, they observe, since those large logs on paper translate very differently into actual walls.

Radiant-heat floors are topped with blue stone in some areas of the home, with random-width pine in others. Lori says the contractor tried to talk them out of pine since the wood is soft and easily marred. No way! No worries! A million dents later, their beat-up floor has real character! Those wear marks map memories too. Take, for instance, the hundred or so dents in the living room. Mickey chuckles, that's where their daughter learned to twirl her wooden baton!

SIGN ON THE DOTTED LINE, PLEASE

Samuel Goldwyn once said, "A verbal contract isn't worth the paper it's written on." And while many artisans still prefer to do business with a handshake, people who have been around the block subscribe to a different reality. No matter how much you trust the person, it is just simply good business to spell everything out in a written contract. Contracts achieve three basic but very important things: they define expectations so that all parties understand their obligations; they create a sense of accountability; and they help to avoid many problems on the job site as a result of up-front planning.

MAIN FLOOR PLAN

DECK

LIVING ROOM
22' X 17'

KITCHEN
15' X 11'

SUNROOM
21' X 15'

CONSERVATORY
7' X 13'

DEN
17' X 13'

DINING
15' X 11'

STORAG

BATH

UP

GUEST ROOM
17' X 10'

ENTRY

GUEST ROOM
15' X 10'

BATH

UTILITY

COVERED ENTRY

GARAGE
25' X 29'

UPPER FLOOR PLAN

OPEN TO BELOW

BEDROOM
14' X 15'

STOR

MASTER BEDROOM
17' X 18'

BATH

MASTER BATH

CLOSET

LOFT
11' X 15'

DN

BEDROOM
14' X 15'

RESOURCES

ARCHITECTS AND DESIGNERS

Bates Timber Design
Mark Bates
PO Box 339
Huntsville UT 84317
801-745-2711
801-745-0638 fax
Bates Timber Design specializes in log and timber materials with a commitment to site-specific designs.

Jack Begrow Architect, AIA
101 West Dixon
Charlevoix MI 49720
213-547-9444
231-547-9462 fax
E-mail: hjaia@netonecom.net
Nationally award-winning log-home designs—you just can't beat experience!

Carney, John and Nancy
Carney Architects
PO Box 9218
Jackson WY 83002
307-733-5546
307-733-1147 fax
E-mail: mailbox@carneyarchitects.com
Web site: www.carneyarchitects.com
A full-service commercial, residential, and resort architecture firm.

Cartrette, Katherine
Mulfinger, Susanka, Mahady &
    Partners, Inc.
904 South 4th Street
Stillwater MN 55082
651-351-0961
651-351-7327 fax
E-mail: stillwater@msmpartners.com
Web site: www.msmpartners.com
A full-service residential architecture firm.

Designing Change
Tom Hahney
7928 Lynwood Drive
Ferndale WA 98248
360-354-5840
360-354-5840 fax
E-mail:
    designing_change@compuserve.com
Providing a complete spectrum of detail design and structural consulting services that are tailored to meet the unique needs of log and heavy-timber structures.

Doty, Michael
Michael Doty Associates, Architects
PO Box 2792
Ketchum ID 83340
208-726-4228
208-726-4188 fax
E-mail: mda@mda-arc.com
A full-service residential, commercial, and resort architectural firm.

Fisher, Richard A., Architects
1932 - 1st Avenue, Ste 502
Seattle WA 98101
206-441-0442
206-728-2318 fax
A quality-oriented design firm specializing in vacation country homes and resorts.

Froncek, Paul, AIA
44 Main Street
Stockbridge MA 01262-0494
413-298-0098
413-298-0099 fax
E-mail: froncekp@aol.com
A small, residential architectural design office specializing in traditional, timber frame, log, and modern structures for clients throughout the United States.

Gibson, David
Gibson * Reno Architects
210 East Hyman Avenue, Ste 202
Aspen CO 81611
970-925-5968
970-925-5993 fax
E-mail: gibsnrno@rof.net
Custom resort development.

Hailey Digital
Richard Sher
PO Box 6364
Ketchum ID 83340
208-788-4922 fax
Utilizing advanced computer technology, this company creates virtual walk-throughs of architectural plans and landscaping to help clients better visualize and design the homes they plan to build.

Hamilton, Paul
Hamilton Home Design
3184 Old Darby Road
Darby MT 59829
406-821-4510 tel/fax
Paul is an experienced technical illustrator who relishes the challenge and fun inherent in log home design.

Hughes, Gordon
Maple Island Log Homes
5046 West Bayshore Drive, Ste A
Suttons Bay MI 49682
800-678-0175
616-271-4541 fax
E-mail: milh@mapleisland.com
Web site: www.mapleisland.com
Builders and designers of unique, handcrafted log residences using massive, Norway red-pine timbers.

Jackobson, Gary
Jacobson and Associates
1161 Skalkaho Road
Hamilton MT 59840
406-363-4089
406-363-2780 fax
E-mail: jake@bitterroot.net
Twenty years of log-structure design.

Log Rhythms, Inc.
Greg and Lee Steckler
20380 Halfway Road, Ste B
Bend OR 97701
541-389-4887
541-389-6833 fax
E-mail: greg@logrhythms.com
Web site: www.logrhythms.com
A full-service computer-aided design firm specializing in log home designs in color, 3-D, or photo rendered. They also produce three-dimensional, computer-generated models and videos of house plans, which can be altered to reflect the look and feel of different design options.

Miller, Park, Architect
2 North Santa Cruz Avenue, Ste 209
Los Gatos CA 95030
408-399-5040
Values one-on-one relationships with individuals and families to meet their unique, residential log-and frame-home needs.

Ruscitto/Latham/Blanton Architectura
Jim Ruscitto
PO Box 419
Sun Valley ID 83353
208-726-5608
208-726-1033 fax
Specializing in the design of rustic mountain-resort architecture throughout the western states.

Wertheimer, Lester
Architectural License Seminars (ALS)
924 Westwood Boulevard, Ste 840
Los Angeles CA 90024
310-208-4646
310-824-7028 fax
E-mail: alsonline@earthlink.net
Web site: www.alsonline.com
ALS offers preparatory training for the architecture registration exam.

Wright, Rick
Wright Design Studio
20380 Halfway Road, Ste B
Bend Oregon 97701
541-389-9178
541-330-1755 fax
Web site: www.wrightdesignstudio.com
Custom home design from concept to completion.

BUILDERS, LOG PRODUCERS, AND SUPPLIERS

Alpine Log Homes
PO Box 85
118 Main Street
Victor MT 59875
406-642-3451
406-642-3242 fax
Offering professional design and engineering, exact logwork costing, graded logs, shipping coordination, guaranteed delivery dates, on-site reassembly supervision, and ongoing construction consultation.

Beck & Associates
Andy Beck
PO Box 4030
Vail CO 81658
970-949-1800
970-949-4335 fax
E-mail: beck_assoc@compuserve.com

Big Timberworks
One Rabel Lane
PO Box 368
Gallatin Gateway MT 59730
406-763-4639
406-763-4818 fax

Bridger Mountain Log Homes
Stan Yung
PO Box 88
561 Business Hub Drive
Belgrade MT 59714
406-388-2030
406-388-2040 fax
A family-owned company specializing in custom-designed, manufactured, and handcrafted log homes. Affiliated with Stan Yung Construction offering on-site building services.

Bullock & Company Master Craftsmen
Elizabeth and Timothy Bullock
PO Box 275
Creemore, ONT Canada L0M 1G0
705-466-2505
705-466-3577 fax
E-mail: bullock@bconnex.net
Web site: www.bconnex.net/~bullock
Designers, builders, and consultants of handcrafted log and timber structures, widely recognized in the industry for their fine execution of intricate heavy-timber roof systems.

Chambers, Robert
Sparwood Homes
N8203 - 1130th Street
River Falls WI 54022
715-425-1739
715-425-1746 fax
E-mail: robert@logbuilding.org
Web site: www.logbuilding.org
Robert Chambers builds log homes, teaches handcrafted log joinery, and writes about the techniques of the craft as depicted in his book Log Building Construction Manual.

Custom Log Homes, Inc.
Drawer 218
3662 Hwy 93 N
Stevensville MT 59870
406-777-5202
406-777-2738 fax
E-mail: sales.connie@customlog.com
Web site: www.customlog.com
Design and construction of hand-hewn, full-round chinked, Swedish-coped, and post-and-beam log homes.

Dembergh, Peter
Dembergh Construction, Inc.
PO Box 3006
Ketchum ID 83340
208-726-2440
208-726-2443 fax
E-mail: dcihomes@sunvalley.net
Web site: home.rmci.net/dcihomes
With 20 years of experience, Dembergh Construction has gained a reputation for crafting fine log homes, timber structures, and traditional country homes.

Foutz, Jere
PO Box 1193
Arnold CA 95223
209-795-5147 (to send a fax, press *51)
Builder of custom log homes.

Frontier Homes, Inc.
Jeff Downey
1225 Willow Creek Road
Corvallis MT 59828
888-593-2257
406-961-8309 fax
Founded over twenty-two years ago, the owners of this small company remain the principal builders of the Shoshone model as well as all their other handcrafted homes.

Guzzi, Ted & Sherry
Timber Design, Inc.
PO Box 7763
Tahoe City CA 96145
530-583-9573
530-583-0567
E-mail: guzzi@inreach.com
Distinctive log homes and interiors.

Haynal, Jim
Jim Haynal Construction
106 Terrace Court
Polson MT 59860
406-883-2065

Hearthstone
120 Carriage Drive
Macon GA 31210
800-247-4442
912-477-6535 fax
E-mail:
    hearthstonehomes@mindspring.com
Web site: www.hearthstonehomes.com
Custom designs, hand-hewn and machine-worked logs, dovetail joinery, and timber-frame construction.

Homan, Kevin
Raven Homes and Furnishings
PO Box 417
Tahoe Vista CA 96148
530-583-0105
Classic and artistic homes, interiors, and furnishings.

Iszler, Elliott
Lonetree Builders
PO Box 161098
Big Sky MT 59716
406-995-2322
406-995-2337 fax
E-mail: lonetree@gomontana.com
Your dreams, our expertise!

Kuhn, Chris
Christopher J. Kuhn Custom Builder
1221 Davis Road
Boyne City MI 49712
616-582-7954
616-582-7078 fax
E-mail: cjk@freeway.net
Custom home buider, specializing in all types of construction.

LaChance, Tom
LaChance Builders
395 Del Rey Road
Whitefish MT 59937
406-862-5597
406-862-8087 fax
E-mail: info@lachancebuilders.com
Web site: www.lachancebuilders.com

Lindal Cedar Homes
4300 South 104th Place
Seattle WA 98178
206-725-0900
206-725-1615 fax
E-mail: sigb@lindal.com
Web site: www.lindal.com
The world's largest and oldest manufacturer of top-quality custom cedar homes and sunrooms.

Logcrafters
Stewart and Mary Thompson
PO Box 1540
Pinedale WY 82941
307-367-2502
307-367-4475 fax
E-mail: logcraft@coffey.com
Web site: www.logcrafters.com
No matter the laser instruments, the pneumatic and electric tools, the cranes or the CAD and engineering equipment, the final joinery is formed by the human hand, a one-of-a-kind work of art.

McNamara, Jack
McNamara Company
PO Box 1250
Sun Valley ID 83353
208-726-2372
208-726-2559 fax
Master builders of unique architecture.

Maple Island Log Homes
5046 West Bayshore Drive, Ste A
Suttons Bay MI 49682
800-678-0175
616-271-4541 fax
E-mail: milh@mapleisland.com
Web site: www.mapleisland.com
Builders and designers of unique, handcrafted log residences using massive, Norway red-pine timbers.

Neville, Mark
Neville Log Homes
2036 Hwy 93
Victor MT 59875
800-635-7911
406-642-3093 fax
E-mail: mark@nevilog.com
Web site: www.nevilog.com
Manufacturer of precut log homes.

Norris & Associates
Chad Yates
PO Box 5759
Snowmass Village CO 81615
970-923-2030
970-923-4639 fax
With over twenty-five years of solid experience as a general contractor in the Colorado Rockies, Norris and Associates has become recognized as "the mountain builder" of choice.

Northwest Custom Log Homes, Inc.
Tresa and Dennis King
17285 Satterlee Way
Bend OR 97707
541-593-5610
541-593-9741 fax
E-mail: logking@cmc.net
Web site: www.nwcustomloghomes.com
An independent custom-handcrafted log home company that brings the grandeur of the forest into a project by uniquely blending cottage industry with our logsmiths wood artistry.

Occidental Log Homes
Tad and Kimberly Horning
5854 Rawhide Court, Ste A
Boulder CO 80302
440-303-8775
303-440-0736 fax
E-mail: occloghome@aol.com
Expertly crafted scribe-fit and chinked log homes.

Omarha, Bill
Omarha Construction
852 Robinwood Court
Traverse City MI 49684
616-947-1982

On Site Management
Michael Riley
417 West Mendenhall Avenue
Bozeman MT 59715
406-586-1500
406-582-1513 fax
E-mail: mike00@in-tch.com
Web site: www.onsitemanagement.com

or

On Site Management
3510 Lake Creek Drive
Jackson WY 83001
307-733-0733
At OSM, we understand the uses of native materials, have a thorough knowledge of modern construction methods, and appreciate the rigorous demands of thoughtful architecture.

Oregon Log Homes
PO Box 1377
Sisters OR 97759
541-549-9354
541-549-1135 fax
E-mail: business@oregonloghomes.com
Web Page: www.oregonloghomes.com
High-quality handcrafted log homes since 1970.

Perma-Chink Systems, Inc.
17635 NE 67th Court
Redmond WA 98052
Call the Log Home Authority line for
    professional advice and guidance:
800-548-1231
425-869-0107 fax
Web site: www.pemachink.com
Everything needed to protect, seal, and beautify your log home, delivered right to your door.

Pioneer Log Homes
Jay Pohley
1344 Hwy 93
Victor MT 59875
406-961-3273
406-961-5647 fax
Pioneer Log Homes of Victor, Montana, is the handcrafted division of Rocky Mountain Log Homes, dedicated since 1976 to the art of combining old-world craftmanship with modern technology.

Rappa, Jerry
Rappa Construction
PO Box 157
St. Germain WI 54558
715-542-3597
715-542-3597 fax
Custom homes and building.

RiverSong Art and Design
Michael Neelin
RR 4
Quoyon, QUE Canada J0X 2V0
819-647-6365
819-647-6365 fax
E-mail: riversong@indelta.com
Web site:
    www.riversong.loghomeshow.com
Since 1984, Michael Neelin of RiverSong Studio has been preparing custom designs of distinctive log homes that grow out of the dreams of their owners and the spirit of the land.

Rocky Mountain Log Homes
1883 Hwy 93 South
Hamilton MT 59840
406-363-5680
406-363-2109 fax
E-mail: sales@rmlh.com
Web site: www.rmlh.com
Rocky Mountain Log Homes has been creating log homes for over three decades, offering a wide range of styles that includes precision-milled, handcrafted, and log-frame homes.

Smith, Burr
Burr Smith Construction
PO Box 783
Hailey ID 83333
208-788-4538
208-788-7020 fax
Commercial and residential construction. We do whatever it takes!

Stopal, Richard
Richard (Log Homes) Stopal
PO Box 1281
Hailey ID 83333
208-788-9693
Custom-handcrafted log homes—all styles of construction.

Thiede, Art
Woody's Log Homes
PO Box 2735
Hailey ID 83333
208-788-4393
208-788-7619 fax
E-mail: thiede@sunvalley.net
Web site: www.loghomesconnect.com
Log home building, restoration, and mainte-nance.

Thistlewood Timber Frame Homes
Scott Murray
RR 6
Markdale, ONT Canada N0C 1H0
800-567-3280
519-986-4461 fax
E-mail: thistle@headwaters.com
Web site: www.interlog.com/~thistle
Award-winning builder of custom timber frame.

Timmerhus, Inc.
Ed Shure
3000 North 63rd Street
Boulder CO 80301
303-449-1336
303-449-9170 fax
Designs and builds handcrafted, scribe-fit log homes and timber-frame structures along with custom doors, windows, and cabinets.

Town and Country Cedar Homes
Stephen Biggs
4772 U.S. 131 South
Petoskey MI 49770
800-968-3178
616-347-7255 fax
E-mail: town@freeway.net
Web site: www.cedarhomes.com
The people of Town and Country have been creating finely crafted wooden homes for over fifty years.

Walkman, Joe
Walkman & Company
59 Marina Road
Yarmouth ME 04096
207-846-3810
207-846-6192 fax
E-mail: lcbond@msn.com
Custom-designed and -built log and traditional framed homes.

Weatherall Northwest
658 Hwy 93 South
Hamilton MT 59840
800-531-2286
406-363-1558 fax
Suppliers of chinking materials, sealants, preservatives, and fine finishes for log homes.

Yung, Stan
Stan Yung Construction
PO Box 88
561 Business Hub Drive
Belgrade MT 59714
406-388-2030
406-388-2040 fax
Stan Yung Construction serves as on-site contractors for the log homes produced by his family-owned company, Bridger Mountain Log Homes.

Zoerhoff, Scott
812 Maple Street
Petoskey MI 49770
616-348-9836
His mother's favorite builder.

INTERIOR DECORATORS, ARTISANS, AND SPECIALIZED DECOR

Damon Design
Gregg Hanzel
155 Auction Road
Kalispell MT 59901
406-257-2565
Specializing in ornamental iron.

Garden Art and Design
Barbara Pressler
PO Box 995
Sandpoint ID 83864
208-265-9288
208-263-2952 fax
A one-of-a-kind landscape and garden artist specializing in unique and customized garden art and design for the discriminating taste. Work has been featured in Country Living Gardener, Organic Gardening *and* Horticulture *magazines and several high-end garden books.*

Golay Masonry
2140 Eldridge
Twin Falls ID 83301
208-734-7728
Quality custom masonry for over 45 years.

Golay's Twin Falls Granite and Marble
2140 Eldridge
Twin Falls ID 83301
208-734-7728
208-734-7795 fax
Fabrication of all kinds of granite and marble countertops.

Hodgins, William
William Hodgins, Inc.
232 Clarendon Street
Boston MA 02116
617-262-9538
617-267-0534 fax

Horne, Colleen
Andover Interior Design West
6362 Vintage Oak Lane
Salt Lake City UT 84121
801-277-2423
801-277-2493 fax
Classic interior design and fine art consulting.

LiteTouch, Inc.
3550 South 700 West
Salt Lake City UT 84119
801-268-8668
801-268-9200 fax
Brilliant solutions in lighting automation.

Metal Works, Inc.
Mark Sheehan
PO Box 1815
Ketchum ID 83340
208-788-5451
Custom metal work.

Moreland, Susie
By Design Interiors, Inc.
623 South First
Hamilton MT 59840
406-363-4473
406-363-1877 fax
Professional design services for the entire home.

Niven, Susan
1440 Stone Canyon Road
Los Angeles CA 90077
310-476-3966
310-472-2789 fax
Interior design from construction to custom design and one-of-a-kind accessories.

Painted Moose, The
Brad Simmons
870 Craintown Road
Gravle Switch KY 40328
606-332-8400
606-332-4433 fax
E-mail: mrbrad@mis.net
Home furnishings and accessories for the rustic lifestyle.

Quiet Moose/Compass Interiors, The
2666 Charlevoix Avenue
Petoskey MI 49770
800-960-0800
616-348-5353 tel
616-348-5362 fax
Professional interior design services and a retail center featuring unique furniture and accessories.

Rain Window & Door Company
Rasen and Jim Guerin
4890 Pearl Street
Boulder CO 80301
303-442-8409
303-442-8409 fax
Handcrafted custom European windows.

Rysso-Peters (cabinetry)
Greg Peters
225 West Deer Valley Road
Phoenix AZ 85027
602-587-9122
602-587-8955 fax
Custom antique-reproduction furniture: "When the ordinary just won't do."

Shirno Cabinets, Inc.
Ole Netteberg
5729 Hwy 93 South
Whitefish MT 59937
406-862-1661
406-862-2707 fax
Specializing in custom cabinetry design and manufacturing for over thirty years.

Sisson, Carole
Carole Sisson Design, ASID
117 East Main
Bozeman MT 59715
406-587-2600
406-587-9651 fax
Interior design studio and showroom.

Southwest Door Company
9280 East Old Vail Road
Tucson AZ 85247
520-574-7374
888-887-2870 fax
Web site: www.southwestdoor.com
Manufacturers of windows, doors, and flooring for the distinctive log home.

StairMeister Log Works LLC
5845 Rawhide Court, Ste. A
Boulder CO 80302
303-440-2994
303-440-0736 fax

Torstenson, Catherine
Interiors by Catherine, Inc.
475 North Main Street
Kalispell MT 59901
406-755-4698
406-755-9698 fax
A Treasure Trove of Creativity.

Wagner, Sherri
Sherri Wagner Interior Design
3746 Rose Crest Drive
Missoula MT 59804
406-728-5504

Woodward Taylor, Emily
Emily Woodward Taylor Decorative
    Painting
1106 East 8175 South
Sandy UT 84094
801-352-0382 fax
E-mail: petiterouge@compuserve.com
Decorative wall prints. Call for more information and to request a catalog.

BOOKS

American Log Homes (1986)
Arthur Thiede and Cindy Teipner,
co-authors (208-788-4393).
Cindy and Art present more than 200 color and black-and-white photographs of the dozens of unique log homes they discovered in their cross-country search of America. Numerous floor plans are also included.

Hands-On Log Homes (1998)
Cindy Teipner Thiede and Art Thiede,
co-authors (208-788-4393).
Beautiful photography highlights unique "built from scratch" homes along with marvelous examples of restorations and imaginative and money-saving uses of recycled materials. Included are the stories and building experiences of involved owners. A handy resource guide provides leads for design, building, manufacturing, and decorating needs.

The Log Home Book (1993)
Cindy Teipner-Thiede and Arthur Thiede,
co-authors (208-788-4393).
This bright, beautiful resource book showcases hundreds of design innovations in the log home industry. It features 200 color photographs of exteriors and interiors of classic and contemporary homes, along with a clearly illustrated section on care, maintenance, and construction.

The previous three books are published by
Gibbs Smith, Publisher
PO Box 667
Layton UT 84041
800-748-5439 to order
801-544-5582 fax
E-mail: info@gibbs-smith.com
Web site: www.gibbs-smith.com

MAGAZINES

Home Buyers Publications
4451 Brookfield Corporate Drive, Ste 101
PO Box 220039
Chantilly VA 22022
800-826-3893
703-222-3209 fax
Publisher of Log Home Living, Log Home Living Annual Buyer's Guide, and Timber Frame Homes magazines. Ideas and resources for consumers who plan to build or buy log or timber-frame homes.

Homestead Communications Corp.
441 Carlisle Drive
Herndon VA 22070
703-471-2041
703-471-1559 fax
Publishers of Country's Best Log Homes magazine, which focuses exclusively on milled log homes.

Log Home Design Ideas
H & S Media
1620 South Lawe Street, Ste 2
Appleton WI 54915
800-573-1900
414-830-1710 fax
Technical building and design information for log home builders and consumers.

Log Homes Illustrated Magazine
Log Homes Illustrated Annual
    Buyer's Guide
GCR Publishing Group
1700 Broadway, 34th Floor
New York NY 10019
212-541-7100
212-245-1241 fax
A complete consumer guide to log homes in North America.

THE INFORMATION NETWORK

Log Homes Connect
Art Thiede
PO Box 2735
Hailey ID 83333
208-788-4393
208-788-7619 fax
E-mail: thiede@sunvalley.net
Web site: www.loghomesconnect.com
Log home design, construction, architectural photography (stock material and on-site shoots), writing, log home tours, and real estate links to available log homes and land throughout the United States. We consult on anything pertaining to log homes.

www.buildingsystems.org
A collection of information related to building in general; however, the site includes a link to the Log Home Council that includes a directory, library, and full information regarding log homes.

www.buildyourownhome.com
Here is a place for sharing owner-builder enthusiasm and ideas. The site also directs you to bargains, helps you solve building problems, and provides opportunity to comment.

www.hometime.com
Based on the Hometime television series, this site contains information relating to log home construction.

www.loghelp.com
Schroeder Log Home Supply
Steve Yakle
34810 U.S. Hwy 2
Grand Rapids MN 55744
800-359-6614
E-mail: syakle@northernnet.com
Web site: www.loghelp.com
This site is geared toward the log home builder or buyer and features specialty products for log homes from chink, hardware, stains, and preservatives to books, videos, and reference materials.

www.loghome.net
Log home resources galore for the log home builder, buyer, and seller.

www.loghomeshow.com
This site provides listings of log home builders throughout North America.

www.tfguild.org//index.html
Produced by the Timber Frames Guild, this site offers information on timber-frame construction and design.

**www.woodworking.com/loghome/
logassoc/index.html**
This site is a good resource for anyone looking for a log builder or for log builders looking for work. It also provides home construction information.

www.woodworking.com/loghomes/
Another source of log home information that covers the usual topics about home construction and offers a BBS (bulletin board system) where you can communicate with others who have similar interests.

SEMINARS AND LOG HOME ORGANIZATIONS

**American/Canadian Log Builders
Association International**
PO Box 775
Lumby BC Canada V0E 2G0
250-547-8776
250-547-8775 fax
E-mail: logassoc@junction.net
Web site: www.logassociation.org
This 27-year-old nonprofit organization is devoted to furthering the art of handcrafted log construction and to promoting the highest standards in the trade. They write and distribute educational material to builders, institutions, and industry. Contact for membership information.

Log Home Living Seminars, Inc.
4200 T
Lafayette Center Drive
PO Box 220039
Chantilly VA 20153
800-826-3893
Web site: www.loghomeliving.com
Homebuyer Publications sponsors four major, three-day regional shows annually along with dozens of one-day, general-information seminars year-round throughout the United States.

Log Homes Council
1201 - 15th Street NW
Washington DC 20005
800-368-5242
Web site: www.loghomes.org
LHC members sponsor research, training, and marketing programs committed to raising industry standards. The council has developed a log home grading and certification program that all member companies must adhere to.